SPORT FOR LIFE

KARATE

Richard J. Schmidt
University of Nebraska—Lincoln

James L. Hesson
Delta State University

Charles B. Corbin/Philip E. Allsen, Series Editors

Scott, Foresman and Company
Glenview, Illinois   Boston   London

SPORT FOR LIFE

AEROBIC DANCE Phyllis C. Jacobson *Brigham Young University*

BOWLING Joyce M. Harrison *Brigham Young University* Ron Maxey

CYCLING Lee N. Burkett/Paul W. Darst *Arizona State University*

GOLF James Ewers *University of Utah*

JOGGING David E. Corbin *University of Nebraska at Omaha*

KARATE Richard J. Schmidt *University of Nebraska at Lincoln*
James L. Hesson *Delta State University*

RACQUETBALL Robert P. Pangrazi *Arizona State University*

STRENGTH TRAINING Philip E. Allsen *Brigham Young University*

TENNIS Anne M. Pittman *Arizona State University*

Charles B. Corbin/Philip E. Allsen, Series Editors

Cover photograph by Robert Drea

Library of Congress Cataloging-in-Publication Data

Schmidt, Richard J. 1947-
   Karate / Richard J. Schmidt, James L. Hesson.
     p. cm.—(Sport for life series)
   Includes index.
   ISBN 0-673-18792-6
   1. Karate. I. Hesson, James L. II. Title. III. Series.
GV1114.3.S334   1989   88-15737
796.8'153—dc19   CIP

Copyright © 1989 Scott, Foresman and Company.
All Rights Reserved.
Printed in the United States of America.

1 2 3 4 5 6 7 - MPC - 93 92 91 90 89 88

Foreword

We are calling this series SPORT FOR LIFE because we believe a sports skills series should be more than just a presentation of the "rules of the game." A popular sport or activity should be presented in a way that encourages understanding through direct experience, improvement through prompt correction, and enjoyment through proper mental attitude.

Over the years, each SPORT FOR LIFE author has instructed thousands of people in their selected activity. We are delighted these "master teachers" have agreed to put down in writing the concepts and procedures they have developed successfully in teaching a skill.

The books in the SPORT FOR LIFE Series present other unique features as appropriate to the featured sport or activity.

The Sport Experience. This is a learning activity that explains and teaches a technique or specific rule. Whether it requires the reader to experience selecting a specific bicycle, stroking a backhand in tennis, or choosing an approach to use in bowling it carries the learner right to the heart of the game or activity at a pace matching his or her own progress. The Sport Experience is identified throughout the book with its own special typographical design.

The Error Corrector. The SPORT FOR LIFE authors have taken specific skills and listed some of the common errors encountered by participants; at the same time they have listed the methods to be utilized to correct these errors. The Error Corrector can be compared to a road map as it provides checkpoints toward skillful performance of a sport or activity.

The Mental Game. Understanding the mental game can remove many of the obstacles to success. The authors have devised techniques to aid the reader in planning playing strategy and in learning how to cope with the stress of competition. It is just as important to know how to remove mental errors as it is to deal with the physical ones.

The editors and authors of SPORT FOR LIFE trust that their approach and enthusiasm will have a lasting effect on each reader and will help promote a lifetime of health and happiness, physically and psychologically, for a sport well played or an activity well performed.

Charles B. Corbin/Philip E. Allsen

About the Authors and Editors

Richard J. Schmidt. Professor Schmidt is an assistant professor in the School of Health, Physical Education, and Recreation at the University of Nebraska, where he received a Distinguished Teaching Award. He is also the director of the Nippon Shobukai at the University of Nebraska—Lincoln. Professor Schmidt is a black belt in karate, kendo, iaido, and naginata. He holds the following yudansha (black belt) grades: Shotokan karate (3rd Dan), kendo (4th Dan), iaido (3rd Dan), and naginata (1st Dan). He is also affiliated with the following martial arts organizations: Nippon Karate-Dō Kenkojuku Association, Kendo Federation of the United States of America, United States Naginata Federation, and the Kokusai Budo Renmei.

Professor Schmidt is a member of the American College of Sports Medicine, Nippon Budo Gakkai, and the Nippon Gaikokujin Budo Kyokai. He is certified as a professional instructor by the Nebraska Law Enforcement Training Center where he teaches defensive tactics for law enforcement personnel.

James L. Hesson. Dr. Hesson is an associate professor at Delta State University in Cleveland, Mississippi. He has been recognized for excellence in teaching at the elementary, junior high, high school, and university levels. For ten years Dr. Hesson has coached championship men's gymnastics teams. He finished his doctoral degree as the valedictorian of his class at Brigham Young University. Dr. Hesson is the author of many articles as well as an author, coauthor, and contributing author of three books. He is a member of the American College of Sports Medicine; the American Alliance of Health, Physical Education, Recreation and Dance; the National Strength and Conditioning Association; Phi Delta Kappa; and the Honor Society of Phi Kappa Phi.

Charles B. Corbin. Dr. Corbin is Professor of Physical Education at Arizona State University. A widely known expert on fitness and health, he is author or coauthor of 27 books addressed to students on those topics ranging from the elementary school through college. In August, 1986, he was given the "Better Health and Living Award" by that magazine as one of ten Americans who have made the difference in influencing others in the areas of health and fitness. He is a 1982 recipient of the National Honor Award from the American Alliance for Health, Physical Education, Recreation and Dance and is a fellow in the American Academy of Physical Education.

Philip E. Allsen. Dr. Allsen is Professor of Physical Education and Director of the Fitness for Life Program at Brigham Young University in Provo, Utah. Widely known for his expertise in physical fitness, sports medicine, and athletic training, Dr. Allsen, a prolific writer, has authored more than 75 articles and written six books covering the topics of strength and physical fitness. The "Fitness for Life" program, which Dr. Allsen developed at Brigham Young University, now serves approximately 7,000 students at the institution each year and has been adopted by more than 400 schools in the United States. He is a member of the American College of Sports Medicine; the American Alliance of Health, Physical Education, Recreation and Dance; and the National Collegiate Physical Education Association.

Preface

This book was written for beginning karate students and for those who teach them. Beginning karate students have many questions and *Karate* contains the answers to many of these early questions, provides a knowledge base, and serves as a reference for individual practice. By using this text as a supplement to karate instruction by a qualified karate teacher, both the student and the teacher can spend more time training and less time talking.

There are many styles of karate. Most of these styles are from Japan, Korea, Okinawa, or China. Each style has its own particular techniques and teaching. Styles are referred to as hard (direct, aggressive) or soft (circular, passive). Some styles emphasize foot techniques while others emphasize hand techniques. *Karate* is an introduction to Japanese Shotokan Karate, which is classified as an aggressive, powerful style. It emphasizes strong blocks and deep attacks using both hand and foot techniques.

As a beginning karate student, you will progress through kihon (basic techniques), kata (formal exercises), and kumite (sparring techniques). Numerous photographs and sequence drawings will help you develop the correct stances and techniques. The Sport Experience will give you practice in learning karate skills and The Error Corrector will help you avoid common mistakes.

You may at first feel overwhelmed by the multitude and complexity of the karate techniques that you need to learn but do not let this discourage you. Continue to push forward in learning your karate techniques and in time you will gradually come to understand not only their nature, but your own as well.

Richard C. Schmidt
James L. Hesson

Contents

1 How to Begin Karate 1
What Is Karate? 1
Why Is Karate a Sport for Life? 1
Where Did Karate Come From? 2
Is Karate the Same Everywhere? 3

2 How to Become a Karateka 5
What Does a Karateka Do? 5
Whet Does a Karateka Wear? 5
Where Does a Karateka Train? 8
How Does a Karateka Behave? 9

3 Kihon (Basic Techniques) 14
The Warm-Up 14
Conditioning 18
Safety 19
Your Weapons 19
Your Targets 21
Physical Principles of Karate Techniques 22
Stances 25
Body Movement 28
Attack and Defense Levels 34
Blocks 36
Punches 42
Kicks 46

4 Kata (Formal Exercises) 53

Ten-No-Kata (Kata of the Universe) 53
Ten-No-Kata Techniques 56
Taikyoku Shōdan 72
Taikyoku Nidan 75
Taikyoku Sandan 75
Heian Shōdan 76
Heian Nidan 80
Heian Sandan 86
Heian Yondan 90
Heian Godan 96

5 Kumite (Sparring) 100

Kumite Principles 100

6 Karate Progress 106

Rank 106
Titles 107
Competition 107

7 Mental Aspects of Karate Training 110

The Code of the Warrior 110
Spiritual and Moral Development 111
The Meaning of Karate-Dō 111
The Principles of Karate-Dō 112

Appendix A Glossary (Japanese/English) 114
Appendix B Pronunciation Guide (Japanese/English) 117
Index 119

How to Begin Karate

Karate begins in your mind. Before you learn any of the physical skills of karate it is important that you understand what karate is, where it came from, and how it should be used.

WHAT IS KARATE?

Karate (Kara = empty, te = hand) is an art and a sport as well as a means of self-defense without weapons.

WHY IS KARATE A SPORT FOR LIFE?

Since karate is an art, a sport, and a means of self-defense, the attraction of karate may be something different for each participant. Karate includes the flowing beauty of the kata and potential violence of self-defense, the stillness of meditation and the blinding speed of movement, the solitude of individual practice and the clamor of competition.

Karate is an activity that appeals to many; crossing boundaries of age, sex, race, occupation, and religion. It may be practiced all year, indoors or outdoors, alone or with a group. No special equipment is required.

In addition to being an activity that offers great variety, it is also an activity that develops physical fitness. In their book, Concepts of Physical Fitness, 6th Edition (Wm. C. Brown, 1987), Corbin and Lindsey have identified eleven aspects of physical fitness: agility, balance, body composition, coordination, cardiovascular endurance, flexibility, muscular endurance, power, reaction time, speed, and strength. When karate training is planned well, it contributes to all of these aspects of physical fitness. Karate also provides an unlimited progression of skill development. No matter what level you reach, there will always be more to learn.

On the basis of physical development alone, karate is an excellent sport for life, yet it offers so much more. In addition to the physical development, karate training includes mental, emotional, spiritual, and moral development. Mentally, karate provides stimulation, challenge, and new knowledge while developing concentration and awareness. Emotionally, karate develops stability, serenity, and inner peace. Spiritually, karate develops a sense of oneness with the universe.

Moral development is an important aspect of karate training. Historically, karate was a form of weaponless self-defense that was taught and practiced only by Buddhist monks. If you are going to learn these powerful skills of self-defense, it is important that you also learn to distinguish between the right and wrong use of these skills. For the great karate masters character development was, and is, the most important aspect of karate training. The following character traits are valued and developed in good karate schools: responsibility for yourself, responsibility for others, discipline, respect, consideration, sincerity, and self-control.

Karate is also a sport for life because it develops self-defense skills that do not require you to carry a weapon. Many places in the world are not safe. We see evidence of violence daily in the news. The crime rate in the United States is high. You may become the victim of a crime at any time. Karate, when practiced as a sport for life, could help you defend yourself.

WHERE DID KARATE COME FROM?

Primitive people learned to fight for survival. Some of the fundamental techniques of karate are as old as the human race. There is evidence of empty-hand fighting techniques existing in Egypt, India, and China 5,000 years ago.

Although karate in its present form is Oriental, it is believed to have originated in India. A Buddhist priest from India, named Bodhidharma, is said to have made the journey from India to China alone and on foot. He began teaching Buddhism at the Shaolin Temple in China during the sixth century A.D. He combined fighting techniques and yoga meditation to unite mind, body, and spirit. The fighting and meditation techniques he taught became known as the Shaolin-Tsu (Shaolin fist way) or Kung Fu. For centuries these techniques were passed from Zen Master to Buddhist monk by word of mouth and in strict secrecy. For hundreds of years these techniques were known only to monks. Eventually the monks began to instruct neighboring farmers so that they could protect themselves against the attacks of bandits. Gradually these fighting techniques spread throughout China. As the Chinese interacted with people from other nations, the techniques spread throughout the Orient, including Okinawa, as early as the fourteenth century A.D. As the art was passed on, variations in technical style and philosophy appeared.

When Japanese feudal lords conquered Okinawa in the seventeenth century A.D., all weapons were taken from the Okinawans and possession of weapons by Okinawans was not allowed. The oppression of this government stimulated an increased popularity of weaponless fighting techniques which were taught, once again, in secrecy.

In 1917 and again in 1922, Gichin Funakoshi was invited to Japan to give demonstrations of Okinawan-te at the Butokuden (hall of martial virtues) in Kyoto and at the National Athletic Exhibition in Tokyo, respectively. As this form of empty-hand fighting gained popularity and developed in Japan, it was modified by Japanese Jujitsu and Korean Tae Kyon.

Tae Kwon Do is the formal name given to modern Korean karate. It is a combination of Korea's ancestral combative arts, Tae Kyon and Subak, and the Kata (formal exercises) of the Okinawan Shuri-te and the Naha-te schools of karate. Tae Kwon Do has been influenced by the spirit of Hwa Rang Do, an educational, military, and social organization for noble youth which was established around 500 A.D. by Jin Heung who was the 24th king of the Silla dynasty. The basic teachings of Hwa Rang Do were loyalty to the nation, respect and obedience to parents, honor to friends, courage and fair play, and avoidance of unnecessary violence.

When Korea was invaded by Japan in the sixteenth century its martial arts were influenced by Chinese Kempo and Japanese Jujitsu. In 1910 Korea was annexed to Japan by force and during the next decades Tae Kyon was further modified by the Okinawan style of Te. In 1945, Korea was liberated from the Japanese and many Korean Dojangs (martial arts schools) were opened under various names. Some Koreans wanted to recover the ancient art of Tae Kyon. Leaders of various schools organized to integrate Tae Kyon with Japanese karate, Chinese Kempo, and Okinawan Te. In 1955, six major schools of Korean karate adopted the name Tae Kwon Do (the art of kicking and punching).

These Oriental forms of fighting were brought to the United States during the late 1940s and the 1950s as American military servicemen returned from Japan, Korea, and Okinawa. The increased interest in these fighting techniques brought experts from each of these countries to demonstrate and teach their style of fighting.

IS KARATE THE SAME EVERYWHERE?

Modern karate is a fusion of many fighting techniques. These techniques have evolved and have been modified for hundreds of years. As a result of hundreds of years of development, the verbal method of passing on information, the large number of teachers throughout its history, the secrecy of various groups, and the different cultures through which it passed, it should not be surprising that there are more than 100 different styles of Japanese karate alone.

In karate, the word *style* refers to the particular system or tradition in which karate is taught. The most well-known forms of empty-hand combat can be classified initially according to nationality such as Japanese, Chinese, Korean, and Okinawan. Within each of these national classifications there are hundreds of styles whose techniques and philosophies vary subtly as a result of continuous changes that have been made in the evolution of each art. Figure 1.1 presents a brief list of some major styles that are prominent today.

Figure 1.1 Major styles of karate

Okinawan	Japanese	Korean	Chinese
Goju-Ryu	Shōtōkan	Tae Kwon Do	T'ai Chi Ch'uan
Isshin-Ryu	Wadō-Ryu	Hapkido	Siu-Lum
Shōrei-Ryu	Shito-Ryu	Tang Soo Do	Hsing-I
Shōrin-Ryu	Goju-Ryu	Taekyon	Wing Chun
Uechi-Ryu	Kyokushinkai		Hop-Gar

In perhaps a hundred major ways these karate styles are all alike and in perhaps a thousand minor ways each is different, just as in a hundred major ways humans are all alike and in a thousand minor ways each of us is different.

In Japan there are approximately 30 styles of karate which designate their teachings as karate-jutsu (empty-hand art or technique). The primary emphasis is self-protection. There are approximately 70 styles of karate which designate their teachings as karate-dō (empty-hand way). The primary emphasis is perfection of character. The "dō" of karate-dō, kendō, judō, aikidō, iaidō, and kyudō translates as "way" or "path" and designates that the practice of the discipline is a way or path to travel throughout life to achieve the ultimate perfection of human character. Japanese karate-dō, when taught properly, is a balanced system of physical education, spiritual discipline, self-defense, and competitive sport.

While the martial arts differ with respect to technique and method, they all serve as systems of education for teaching the values and virtues embodied in the legacy of the samurai warrior of feudal Japan.

How to Become a Karateka

Who is a karateka? A karateka is a person who participates in karate.

WHAT DOES A KARATEKA DO?

Karate is divided into three general areas of training: kihon (basic techniques), kata (formal exercises), and kumite (sparring).

Kihon training is the basic training of all stances, blocks, strikes, punches, and kicks. Practice on these individual skills will usually focus on one skill or technique at a time with an emphasis on precise technical execution. Kihon training is of major importance to every karateka, regardless of skill level.

Kata training is the performance of prearranged sequences of attack and defense. These sequences are performed against imaginary opponents. During the performance of a kata the emphasis is on mastery of execution, which includes correct speed, power, balance, technique, breathing, and body movement. Beyond these physical requirements a kata must also be performed with intensity and feeling. To advance from one rank to the next in karate the performance of at least one kata is required. The kata for each successive rank is more difficult than the preceding one.

Kumite training requires the application of your karate techniques against a real opponent. These are the same skills that you learn and practice in kihon and kata. Kumite training includes prearranged sparring and free-sparring.

These three areas of karate training are covered in greater detail in the later chapters in this book.

WHAT DOES A KARATEKA WEAR?

During karate training the karateka wears a uniform called a gi (gē). The gi consists of an uwagi (jacket), zubon (pants), and obi (belt). The gi is usually white; however, some styles or schools of karate may use a different color. The fabric is either all cotton or cotton/polyester. These uniforms are manufactured in light, medium, and

THE SPORT EXPERIENCE

Using the chart in Figure 2.1, determine what size gi would be correct for you.

Figure 2.1 Clothing size chart

Size	Measurements		Jacket length	Pants length	Belt length
0	For children		28"	26½"	77"
1	Under 4'9"	Less than 105 lbs.	30½"	29"	79½"
2	4'10"-5'3"	106-120	36"	31½"	88"
3	5'4"-5'6"	121-135	38"	34"	95½"
4	5'7"-5'9"	136-165	39½"	37½"	102"
5	5'10"-6'	166-200	40"	39"	111"
6	6'1"	200 & over	50½"	41½"	120"

heavy weight material, as well as in several different sizes. Your gi should fit loosely and should not restrict your movement. Your teacher should be able to help you select the right size. The size chart in Figure 2.1 may also be helpful.

When you put on the uwagi (jacket), the left lapel is folded over the right lapel. A dōjō patch or association patch may be worn on the left breast of the uwagi.

The obi (belt) is looped around your waist and tied in front in a square knot according to the following procedure: fold your belt in half to find the center, place the center of your belt at the center of your waist in front of your body, wrap the belt around your waist until both ends are in front of your body again, and tie a square knot. The ends of your belt should be even in length after the knot is tied. Figure 2.2 shows the correct step-by-step procedure for tying the belt.

The color of your obi depends upon your karate rank. Beginners wear a white belt and the most advanced karateka wear a black belt. Different styles of karate may use different colors in between the white belt and the black belt. Figure 2.3 (page 8) presents one example of belt colors and ranks for a Japanese style of karate.

Your karate gi should always be clean and should not have any holes or tears. It is your responsibility to check your gi before each training session to make sure it is suitable for training. Wear a clean gi to class every day. When you are wearing your gi do not sit in a chair or lean against a wall or any other object.

Never wear shoes on the training surface of the dōjō even if you are in your regular clothes. While training, do not wear shoes, restrictive clothing, or jewelry.

Using a karate belt, practice putting the belt on and tying the knot correctly.

Figure 2.2 Procedure for tying the karate belt

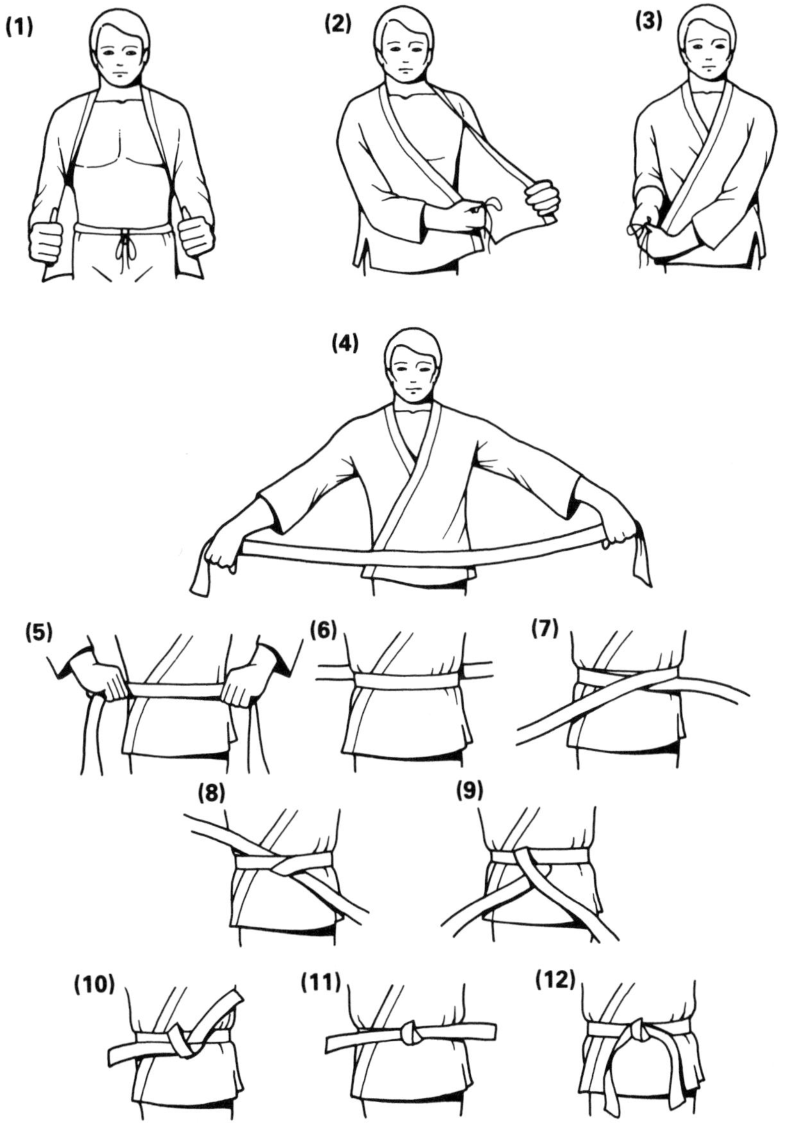

Figure 2.3 Belt colors and ranks

Grade	Color of belt	Japanese names	Degree	Color of belt	Japanese names
10	white	Ju kyū	1	black	Shōdan
9	white	Ku kyū	2	black	Nidan
8	yellow	Hachi kyū	3	black	Sandan
7	green	Shichi kyū	4	black	Yōdan
6	green	Rok kyū	5	black	Godan
5	blue	Go kyū	6	black	Rokudan
4	purple	Yon kyū	7	black	Shichidan
3	brown	San kyū	8	black	Hachidan
2	brown	Ni kyū	9	black	Kudan
1	brown	Ik kyū	10	black	Judan

WHERE DOES A KARATEKA TRAIN?

A karateka trains in a martial arts place or training hall called a dōjō. Loosely translated, it is a place (jō) to practice the way (dō), or a "place of enlightenment." Following the Zen belief of teaching for enlightenment, the dōjō is a place where you experience physical and mental austerities. It is the teacher's responsibility to create this strict, serious, rigorous atmosphere. This training atmosphere will help you to attain your karate goals. The dōjō is more than a training hall, it is a death ground for one's ego. In order for you to grow in karate, it is necessary to get rid of your self-centered and selfish thoughts and behaviors.

A dōjō should be clean and simple. A natural wood floor is preferred. This is in keeping with the Japanese idea of beauty which includes "wabi" (simplicity) and "sabi" (rusticity). A dōjō should not be filled with bright colors, trophies, or excessive ornamentation.

During its development, karate training has become intertwined with Japanese culture. Therefore, most of the dōjō in Japan have a Shintō or Buddhist focal point. The dōjō is a sacred place in which all actions center around the kamidana (dōjō altar). Near the kamiza (upper seat) there is a tokonoma (alcove) housing the dōjō shrine. The shrine normally consists of a hanging kakemono (scroll) and usually some art object such as a fine sword or perhaps a flower. Figure 2.4 shows a typical floor plan of a dōjō.

While most of the dōjō in Japan have a Shintō or Buddhist orientation, dōjō in other countries may use alternative symbols such as a national flag. The presence of the dōjō is recognized and created by a series of ritual acts which focus on "reigi saho" (etiquette). The rituals that are followed have a purpose in karate, but it is not religious conversion. These rituals help you develop the correct attitude toward training, prepare for the learning process, and show respect for the karate tradition.

The environment in which karate training takes place is an important part of establishing the proper attitude that is necessary for concentration. If no formal dōjō exists it is necessary for you to conduct yourself according to specific etiquette and ritual so that boundaries may be set within which you will be able to train your body and your spirit.

Figure 2.4 The dōjō

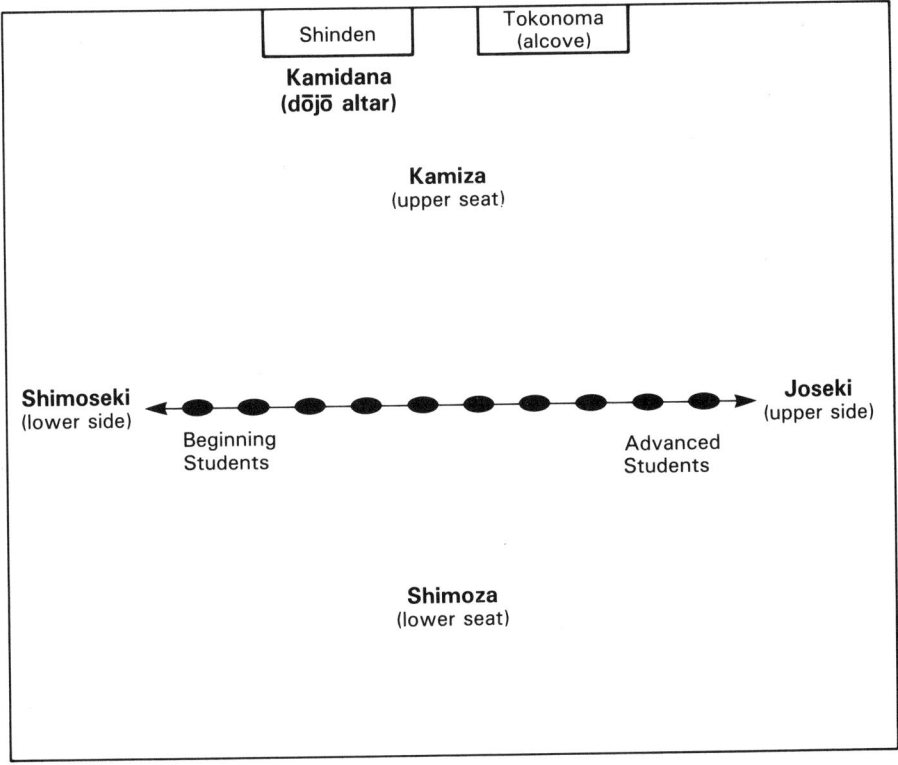

HOW DOES A KARATEKA BEHAVE?

Dōjō protocol and etiquette function to create an environment that is conducive to disciplined training according to Japanese customs and traditions. Although the specific rules of propriety vary from one dōjō to another, there is general agreement concerning behavior in a dōjō.

The traditional dōjō is considered a sacred place, somewhat like a church, in which all behavior should be governed accordingly. Always come to the dōjō with a clean body and a clean gi. Profanity, loud talking, laughing, socializing, and misbehavior are out of place in a dōjō. Do not engage in idle talk in the dōjō. Use your time wisely to develop your body and mind; either train or meditate. Do not disturb the concentration of others. Maintain complete silence when you are watching others perform. During kumite (sparring), broken concentration can result in serious injury.

Karate training demands courtesy. Show respect for your dōjō, your teachers, and your fellow students. Always be courteous and helpful to one another.

The first form of propriety you should learn is the proper way to bow from the standing position and from the seated position. Bowing is the oriental way of greeting and showing respect.

When you enter and leave the dōjō you should bow to the kamidana (dōjō altar) as a gesture of respect for the place where you train, for those with whom you train, and for those who are your teachers.

When you bow toward the front of the dōjō at the beginning and end of your training session you are showing that you are sincere in relinquishing your ego and humbling yourself so that you will be able to learn what is taught. You are also demonstrating a sincere desire to commit yourself to this training session.

Bow to your sensei (teachers) as a greeting and to thank them for being in the dōjō to teach you. Bow to your sempai (seniors) as a greeting.

Bow to your sensei and your opponent before and after kumite (sparring). When you bow to your training partners you are thanking them for being there to help you learn.

Never let this bow of respect become a purely mechanical motion or your training will also become shallow and superficial. Always try to "bow from your heart," with meaning and sincerity. Bow slightly lower when bowing to a superior.

To perform the standing bow (tachirei) start in the following position: body erect, heels together, feet turned out at a 45-degree angle, arms at your sides, fingers together, palms of your hands held firmly against the side of your legs. Keeping your head and torso erect, bend forward at the hips to about a 15-degree angle. Hold your bow at this angle for about one second, then return to the starting position. This bow should never be executed rapidly. Remember to "bow from your heart" to express your sincerity. The formal command to bow is "rei."

To perform a bow from seiza (formal sitting or kneeling position) start in the following position: sit on your feet in a kneeling position, your head and spine should be erect, your hands on top of your thighs. Keeping your spine in a straight line lean forward from your hips and place your right hand, then your left hand on the floor. With your thumbs and index fingers touching each other, bend your upper body forward to a position parallel with the floor. Do not bow deeper than parallel and do not bend your neck so that the back of your neck is exposed to the front of the dōjō. To return to the starting position, first withdraw your left hand, then your right hand, and raise your upper body to the erect sitting position. To stand up from the seiza position, step forward with your right foot, then your left foot, and stand up.

Your position in the dōjō is determined by rank and seniority. The teacher is located closest to the kamidana (dōjō altar) while the students are farthest from the kamidana. As viewed from a position facing the kamidana, the advanced or senior students (sempai) sit to the right and front while the beginning or junior students sit to the left and rear. The jōseki (upper side of the dōjō) is normally reserved for visiting dignitaries while the shimoseki (lower side) is for visitors of lesser rank. You should allow seniors to enter and leave the dōjō first.

At the beginning and at the end of class you will line up according to rank. If you are in the second or third row, line up directly behind someone in the row

THE SPORT EXPERIENCE

Practice your karate bow as shown in Figure 2.5 in front of a mirror so you can check for correct body position. Note both the front position (2) and the side position (3) of the karate bow.

Figure 2.5 The karate bow
(1) (2) (3)

ahead of you. Everyone will then kneel on the floor in seiza (formal sitting position). During zazen (meditation) clear your mind of all worldly thoughts and concerns in preparation for receiving new information. From the seiza position you will bow, as a group, to the kamidana, to the sensei, and to the sempai, in that order.

If your teacher is wearing a gi in the dōjō refer to your teacher as sensei, whether you are dressed in a gi or not. Refer to the other black belts and ranking students who are instructing as sempai.

If you need to talk to your sensei during class and your sensei is busy with someone else, or is training, do not interrupt. Stand at attention, close enough to

How to Become a Karateka

THE ERROR CORRECTOR

After performing a bow, answer the following questions:
1. Did you start with your body erect?
2. Were your heels together?
3. Were your feet turned out at a 45-degree angle?
4. Were your arms at your sides?
5. Were your fingers together?
6. Were the palms of your hands held firmly against the sides of your legs?
7. Did you keep your head and torso in a straight line and bend forward from the hips?
8. Did you stop at a 15-degree angle?
9. Did you hold your bow for one second?
10. Did you bow slowly, with feeling and sincerity?

---

make it clear that you are waiting to speak, but far enough away so that you will not appear to be listening to their conversation or will not interfere with their training. If, within a reasonable length of time, your sensei does not acknowledge your presence, return to your training and speak with your sensei later, unless it is a genuine emergency.

When asking questions begin with "sensei" or "sempai." After you receive a reply say "Thank you, sensei" or "Thank you, sempai." The feeling of kansha (thankfulness) between the student and the teacher is crucial. If you are performing a technique when your sensei answers a question or makes a comment to you, stay where you are. If you are not performing a technique, bow to your sensei and return to your training.

When you are receiving instructions stand relaxed, but erect and attentive, with your feet together and your hands at your sides. Do not scratch, cough, yawn, slouch, or put your hands on your hips. Always be attentive during training and approach every practice with an open, inquisitive mind.

When your sensei tells you to practice a particular technique and goes away to help someone else, practice the technique you have been given until your sensei returns, even if it is an hour. Do not stop to talk as soon as you begin to feel tired. Do not practice different techniques. Follow instructions exactly.

During class instructions never contradict, argue with, or otherwise challenge your sensei or sempai. If you wish to express a difference of opinion see them after class.

Never leave the dōjō during practice without permission from your sensei or sempai. Break time is not intended for socializing; use the time to rest and recover. You may perform slow stretching exercises or quietly watch others train.

When you visit another dōjō, bow to the sensei and sempai, give your name, give your sensei's name, your dōjō, and your rank. Request permission to watch or to train and also request a review of proper protocol at this dōjō. Be courteous and respectful, remember that you are a guest.

Kihon (Basic Techniques)

The basic techniques of karate include blocks, punches, and kicks. These basic techniques require precise, coordinated body movement. All of your blocks, punches, and kicks will be more effective if they are executed in a powerful manner from a stable stance.

Learning some of the physical principles that apply to karate techniques, some of your body's most effective weapons, and some of your best targets, will make your blocks, punches, and kicks more effective.

Physical conditioning is essential to the development of powerful karate techniques. During your training and conditioning there are certain safety guidelines that should be followed to keep you and your training partners from being injured. After all, one of the major reasons for learning karate is to keep from being injured. Each karate training session should begin with a warm-up.

THE WARM-UP

Before participating in vigorous physical activity you should warm up. There are two primary objectives of a warm-up. The first objective is to gently stretch the soft tissues that may restrict your range of motion during exercise. Stretching the muscles will increase your range of motion and decrease the risk of injury to these tissues during vigorous karate training. The second objective of your warm-up is to raise the temperature of these same soft tissues, especially muscle tissue, to improve their performance during activity.

Start with a total body stretch in which all of the major muscles will be stretched. Some general guidelines for the stretching part of your warm-up are: use slow static stretch to the point where you feel a good stretch (not painful, however); hold this stretch for a period of ten to thirty seconds; repeat each stretching exercise one to three times. *Caution:* any stretching exercise can cause injury if the soft tissues of the body are stretched too far. To minimize the risk of injury: always move into stretching exercises gently, only go as far as necessary for you to feel a good stretch.

WARM-UP EXERCISES

Perform the warm-up stretching exercises that follow.

Neck

Bend your head forward so that the muscles on the back of your neck are gently stretched. Bring your head back to a neutral or vertical position, then tilt your head to the right gently stretching the muscles on the left side of your neck. Bring your head back to the neutral position, then tilt your head back gently stretching the muscles on the front of your neck. Bring your head to the neutral position, then tilt your head to the left stretching the muscles on the right side of your neck.

Return your head to a neutral vertical position, then gently turn your head to the right as far as possible and hold this position, do not bounce or jerk. Now gently turn your head to the left as far as possible and hold this position.

Trunk

Gently bend forward as far as you can toward a toe-touch position and let your upper body hang relaxed. Bend your knees slightly and return to a standing position. Stretch both arms overhead, grasp your left wrist with your right hand and lean to your right stretching the muscles along the left side of your body. Return to a neutral standing position, interlock the fingers of both hands, place your arms directly overhead with your palms facing upward, and gently lean back stretching the muscles along the front of your body. Return to a neutral standing position and grasp your right wrist with your left hand, then lean to your left stretching the muscles along the right side of your body.

With your arms extended out from the sides of your body at shoulder level, gently twist your body as far as it will go to the right and hold this position; do not bounce. Come back to neutral and twist your body as far as possible to the left and hold this position; do not bounce.

Shoulders

Place both hands behind your back and interlock your fingers. Keep your elbows straight and raise your hands and arms as high as possible behind your back, stretching the muscles on the front of the shoulder joint. Raise your right arm overhead, bend your elbow so that your right forearm is behind your head, grasp your right elbow with your left hand, and try to pull your right upper arm behind your head. Raise your left arm overhead, bend your elbow so that your left forearm is behind your head, grasp your left elbow with your right hand, and try to pull your left upper arm behind your head.

Elbows and Wrists

Assume a position on your hands and knees with the palms of your hands on the floor, your fingers pointing toward your knees, and your elbows straight. Gently lean back with your shoulders until you feel the stretch on the front side of your forearms. Next, turn your hands over so that the back side of your hands are on the floor with your fingers pointing toward your knees. Keeping your elbows straight, gently lean back until you feel the stretch on the back of your forearms.

Hips

From a standing position, keep your body erect and carefully place your feet as far apart as possible. In this straddle position stretch the muscles along the inside of your thighs. Turn your hips and shoulders to the right so that your right leg is extended in front of your body and your left leg is extended behind your body. Stretch the muscles along the back of your right leg and the front of your left hip. Return to a straddle position and bend forward at the hip joint, keeping your back flat. Stretch the muscles along the inside of your thighs. Turn your hips and shoulders to the left so that your left leg is extended in front of your body and your right leg is extended behind your body. Stretch the muscles along the back of your left leg and the front of your right hip.

Knees

Assume a sitting position with both feet extended in front of your body. With your legs together and your knees straight, lean forward as far as you can and hold that position, stretching the muscles along the back of your body. Return to a sitting position with both legs in front of your body. Bend your left leg so that your left foot is near your left hip but your left knee is still in front of your body. Gently lean back with your upper body until you feel the stretch along the front of your left thigh. Return to a sitting position with both legs in front of your body. Bend your right leg so that your right foot is near your right hip but your right knee is still in front of your body. Gently lean back with your upper body until you feel the stretch along the front of your right thigh.

Ankle

In a standing position place your left foot two feet behind your right foot. Keep both feet flat on the floor and pointing straight ahead. Shift your weight to your left foot and bend your left knee until you feel the stretch on the back of your left ankle joint; hold this position. Shift your weight forward to your right foot, roll the toes of your left foot under until the upper surface of your toes is against the floor. Press down and forward with your left knee until you feel the stretch on the front side of the left foot and ankle.

In a standing position place your right foot two feet behind your left foot. Keep both feet flat on the floor and pointing straight ahead. Shift your weight to your right foot and bend your right knee until you feel the stretch on the back of your right ankle joint; hold this position. Shift your weight forward to your left foot, roll the toes of your right foot under until the upper surface of your toes is against the floor. Press down and forward with your right knee until you feel the stretch on the front side of the right foot and ankle.

THE ERROR CORRECTOR

After performing the warm-up stretching exercises answer the following questions:

1. Did you use slow static stretch?
2. Did you reach a point of moderate discomfort in the muscles being stretched?
3. Could you feel the muscles that were being stretched?
4. Did you hold each stretch for at least ten seconds?
5. Did you avoid bouncing movements during the stretching exercises?

Hold this position or ease up if it begins to hurt, and if an exercise causes you pain find another exercise to replace it. When stretching is done properly it should feel good.

After you have stretched all of the major joints and muscles of your body you have achieved the first objective of a warm-up. The second objective is to increase body temperature. When the soft tissues of the body are warm they are more pliable and this reduces your resistance to movement and the risk of soft tissue damage while increasing your range of motion. There is also some evidence that warm muscle tissue performs better. Almost any total body activity may be used to warm your muscles. Your muscle contractions during this activity are important since approximately 75 percent of the energy released during muscle contraction is converted to heat energy. Almost any type of active calisthenic exercise performed repetitiously will warm the muscles that are used. An excellent way to warm the muscles would be to slowly perform basic karate techniques or a kata. "Breaking a sweat" or the onset of perspiration during physical activity is a good general indication that you are warmed up and ready for more vigorous training.

CONDITIONING

Karate training will contribute to many aspects of total physical conditioning. However, if you wish to further increase your fitness level and improve your karate performance the following guidelines will be helpful.

Strength. Strength refers to the amount of force that a muscle can exert. To develop strength that would be most useful in karate you should perform exercises that involve movement through a full range of motion against resistance, use a resistance that is 70 to 100 percent of your maximum voluntary contraction (one repetition maximum), execute one to ten repetitions, perform each exercise for one to three sets, and repeat your strength training program three days per week with at least 48 hours rest between strength workouts.

One strength program that has sound scientific and practical support is a weight training program in which you perform three sets of six repetitions, using the heaviest weight you can lift six times. This strength workout should be repeated three times a week.

Muscle Endurance. Muscle endurance is the ability of your muscles to exert force for many repetitions or to hold a position for an extended period of time. To develop muscle endurance for karate you should perform exercises that involve movement through a full range of motion against resistance, use a resistance that is 50 to 70 percent of your maximum voluntary contraction (one repetition maximum), execute twenty to thirty repetitions, perform each exercise for one to three sets, and repeat your muscle endurance exercise program three days per week.

Flexibility. Flexibility refers to the range of motion available at a joint. To develop flexibility for karate you should use slow static stretch exercises, stretch to the point of moderate discomfort, hold each stretch for ten to thirty seconds, perform each stretch one to three times, and repeat your stretching program three to seven days per week.

Cardiovascular Endurance. Cardiovascular endurance is your ability to continue vigorous activity for relatively long periods of time. To develop cardiovascular endurance for karate you should perform exercises that use large muscle groups in a rhythmic and continuous manner, exercise at an intensity that will result in a heart rate that is 70 to 85 percent of your estimated maximum heart rate (estimated maximum heart rate equals 220 minus your age), maintain this exercise heart rate for fifteen to sixty minutes, and repeat this cardiovascular endurance workout three to seven times per week.

Body Composition. Body composition refers to what your body is composed of. A particular concern is how much of your body weight is stored body fat. Everyone needs some stored body fat; it is a good thing. However, some people have accumulated too much of a good thing and it is no longer good or healthy. To remove excess body fat it is best to stay on a balanced diet but reduce your total caloric intake. It is also helpful to increase your activity level. The combination of eating less and exercising more will produce a daily caloric deficit that will require the use of your stored body fat as an energy source. To reduce your body composition you should perform exercises that use large muscle groups in a rhythmic and continuous manner, exercise at a heart rate that will produce a cardiovascular training effect (70 to 85 percent of your estimated maximum heart rate), maintain this exercise heart rate for thirty to sixty minutes, and repeat this body composition workout five to seven days per week.

SAFETY

Keep your fingernails and toenails trimmed. Do not wear jewelry or shoes during karate training. Do not wear glasses or contact lenses when sparring. If you must wear glasses or contact lenses during training be sure that you also wear an appropriate eye protection device. To protect your mouth and teeth wear a mouth guard during kumite (sparring). Other than your mouth guard, you should not have anything in your mouth during training such as tobacco, gum, or candy. *Block all face attacks.*

When you are performing attack and defense techniques with an aite (opponent) say "chūi" (warning) before attacking. Wait for your opponent to reply "chūi" before starting your attack. This is a courtesy as well as a means of reducing the possibility of injury.

In the unusual event that you receive an injury requiring immediate treatment, bow to your opponent and bring the injury to the attention of your sensei (teacher).

YOUR WEAPONS

Various parts of your body may serve as weapons. For these weapons to be effective you must first recognize where they are located, then you must train long and hard to make them effective. The following are some of your weapons (see the corresponding numbers in Figure 3.1).

Figure 3.1 Your weapons

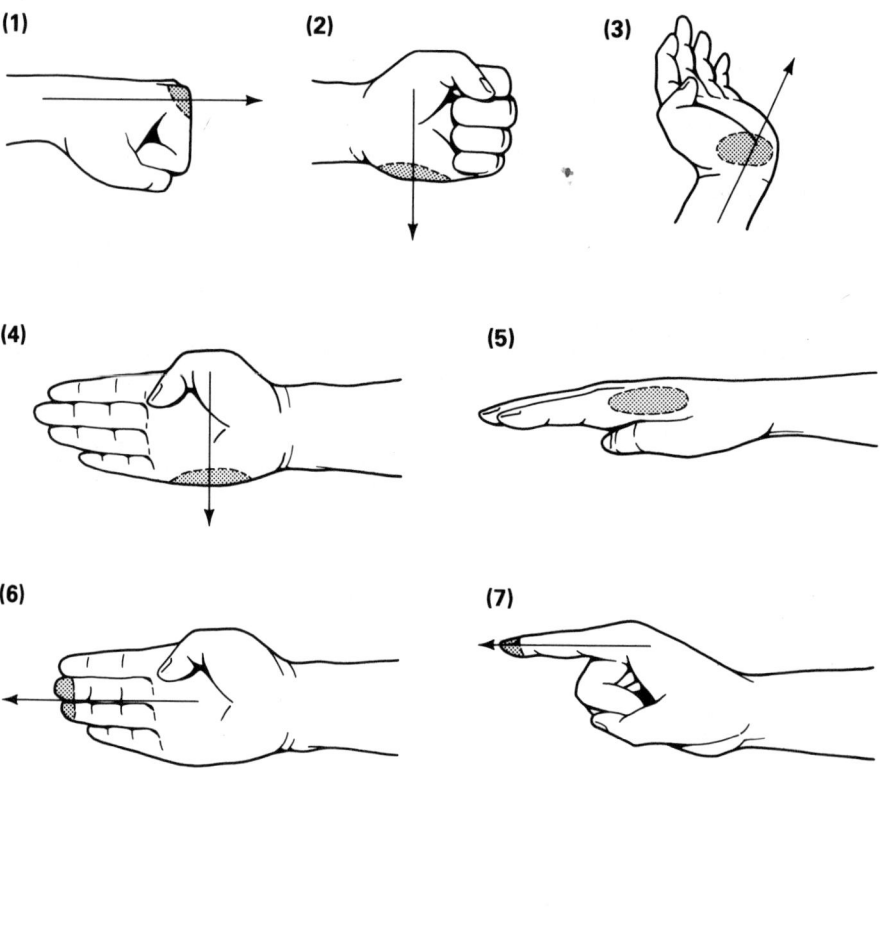

1. Seiken (forefist)
2. Kentsui (hammer fist)
3. Teishō (heel of palm)
4. Shūtō (sword hand)
5. Haitō (ridge hand)
6. Nukite (spear hand)
7. Ippon Nukite (spear finger)
8. Empi (elbow) forward or backward
9. Empi (elbow) up or down
10. Hizagashira (knee)
11. Haisoku (instep)
12. Koshi (ball of foot)
13. Kakatō (heel of foot)
14. Sokutō (sword foot)

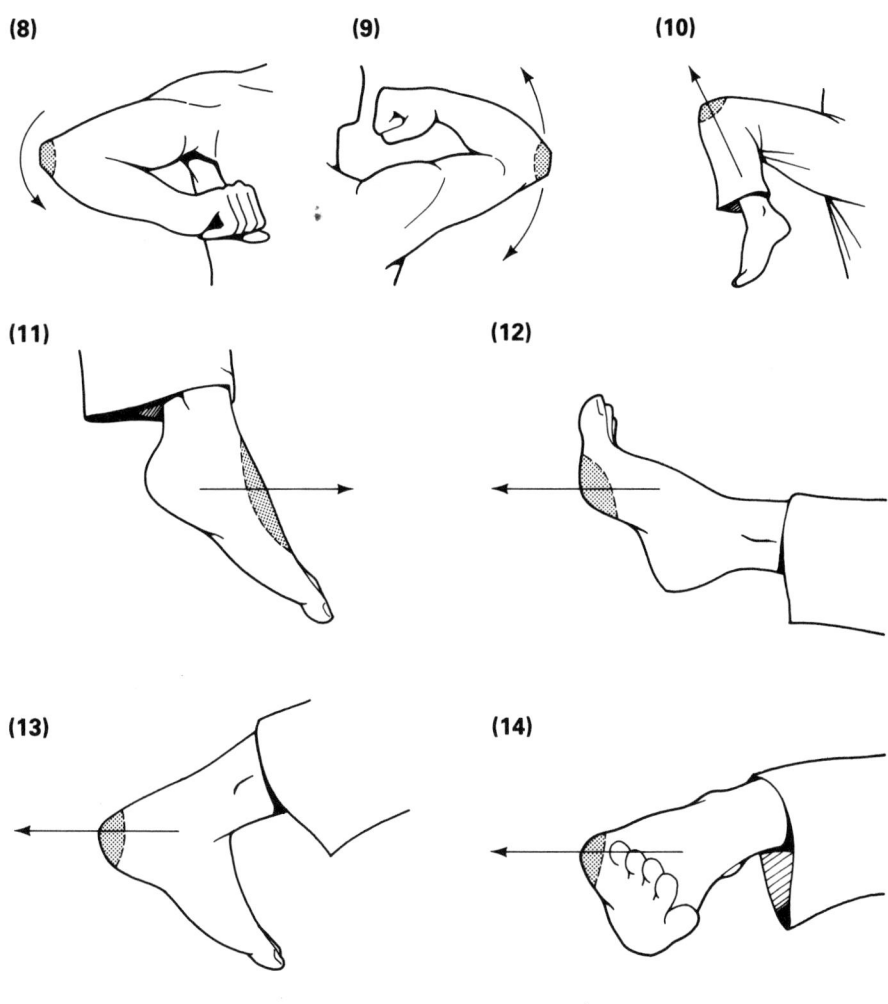

YOUR TARGETS

One of the original purposes of karate was self-defense without weapons. A focused attack can kill or cripple an attacker with one blow. The monks who developed karate did not intend for it to be used to wilfully harm others, but rather so that they could protect themselves if they were attacked. If you are attacked, and there is absolutely no way to avoid a physical conflict, you should defend yourself and counterattack swiftly and with great force. A highly trained karateka should be able to end an attack with one swift, powerful, focused counterattack.

It is important that this counterattack be aimed at a vital target on your attacker's body. Striking a heavily muscled part of the body is seldom effective. Your defense and counterattack will be much more effective if you make forceful contact with a vital target. The following are some of the vital targets on the human body which correspond to the numbers indicated on Figure 3.2.

1. Temple
2. Side of neck
3. Collarbone
4. Armpit
5. Abdomen
6. Testicles
7. Knee
8. Shin
9. Bridge of nose
10. Eye
11. Just below nose
12. Chin
13. Throat
14. Solar plexus
15. Front of elbow
16. Ribs
17. Ankle
18. Back of elbow
19. Wrist
20. Side of knee
21. Instep
22. Skull
23. Back of neck
24. Center of back
25. Kidneys
26. Coccyx
27. Back of thigh
28. Back of knee
29. Achilles tendon

PHYSICAL PRINCIPLES OF KARATE TECHNIQUES

The successful use of karate techniques depends upon the accurate application of force. Correct form in karate is based upon physical principles. The following are a few applications of some physical principles that are useful in karate.

Balance

1. To be balanced, your center of gravity must be within the boundaries of your base of support. You must keep your body weight directly above your supporting foot or feet.
2. To strike with force you need to be in a very stable stance.
3. To move quickly you need to be in an unstable stance.
4. The smaller your base of support the less stable your stance (Example: standing on one foot). The larger your base of support the more stable your stance (Example: standing on both feet placed well apart).
5. The higher your center of gravity is above your base of support the less stable your stance. The lower your center of gravity the more stable your stance.

Figure 3.2   Your targets

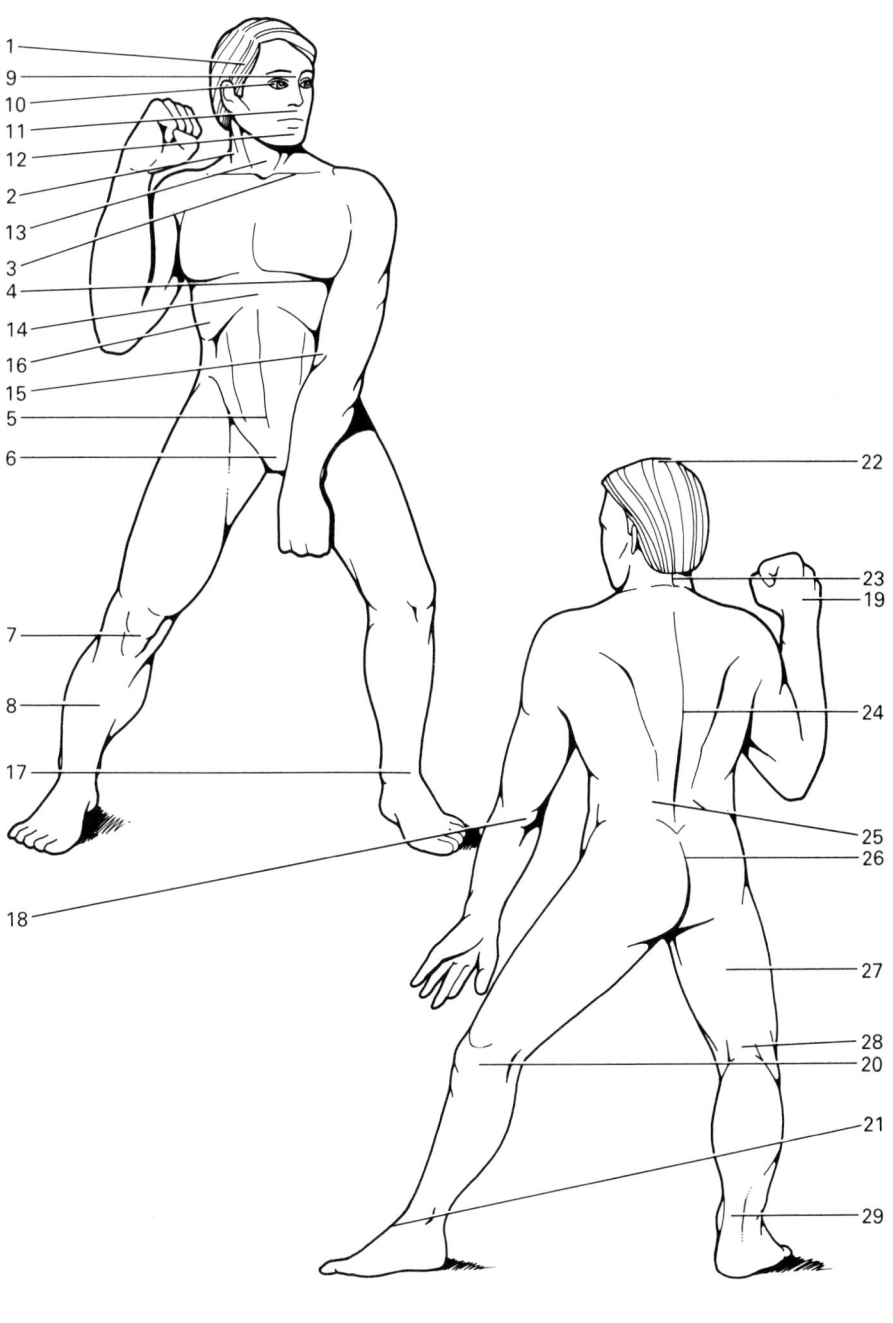

Kihon (Basic Techniques)

6. The lighter your body weight the less stable your stance. This is good for quick movement. The heavier your body weight the more stable your stance. This is good for striking with force.
7. The closer your center of gravity is to the edge of your base of support the less stable your stance. This is good for quick movement. The closer your center of gravity is to the center of your base of support the more stable your stance. This is good for striking with force.
8. Your center of gravity is constantly moving in karate, therefore, your stability is dynamic. Strive for instability when you need to move quickly and stability when you need to strike with force.

Power

1. Your striking power is a product of speed and strength. Increasing either or both will result in an increase in your total striking power.
2. Strike with as much speed as possible. This will increase your total striking power as well as your chances of making contact before your opponent can move or block your attack.
3. The fastest strike is a straight line to the target.
4. The greater the distance over which you can accelerate your striking body part the greater will be your total speed at impact. However, the disadvantage is that long striking movements are easier for your opponent to see and avoid. Strike quickly.
5. The greater the force of your muscle contractions the greater your striking power.
6. Your greatest striking force comes from the largest muscles in your body which are located in your hips and thighs. Your total striking force is the result of sequential muscle contractions from the large central muscles to the smaller muscles of the arms and legs.
7. The force from all of the muscle contractions in your entire body should be directed toward the target for maximum impact.
8. Strike with your entire body weight instead of merely the weight of one hand or one foot.
9. Since there is an equal and opposite reaction to every action, your body needs to be rigid and in a stable stance to ensure that your opponent receives your maximum striking force, and that the reaction force is transferred through your rigid body to the ground.
10. Exhale forcefully and tense all of your muscles at the instant of impact so that your body will be rigid.
11. A muscle that is put on a slight stretch immediately prior to contraction can contract more forcefully. Correct technique in karate provides this pre-stretch whenever possible. Learn your karate techniques exactly as they are taught.
12. Your total striking force should be concentrated upon a small target area and delivered by a small striking area to produce the greatest pressure at impact. Concentrate your total striking power through a small striking area such as one heel or one knuckle.

Figure 3.3 Yōi position

STANCES

Most karate training activities begin with a bow. After the bow you will assume the yōi (ready) position. All basic offensive and defense movements are initiated from this ready position. To get into the yōi position slide your left foot to your left until your feet are shoulder width apart. At the same time, rotate your fists outward in a circle using your elbows as the center of rotation. Your fists should finish in front of your thighs with the palm side toward your body. Figure 3.3 illustrates the yōi position.

Some of the other stances you will use are listed below. These are illustrated in Figure 3.4 (pages 26–27).

1. Heisoku-dachi (formal attention stance)
2. Musubi-dachi (informal attention stance)
3. Hachinoji-dachi (yōi stance)
4. Heikō-dachi (parallel yōi stance)
5. Uchi Hachinoji-dachi (inverted yōi stance)
6. Zenkutsu-dachi (front stance) front view

7. Zenkutsu-dachi (front stance) side view
8. Kōkutsu-dachi (back stance) front view
9. Kōkutsu-dachi (back stance) side view
10. Shiko-dachi (square stance)
11. Kiba-dachi (horse stance)
12. Fudō-dachi (rooted or immovable stance)
13. Hangetsu-dachi (wide hourglass stance)
14. Sanchin-dachi (narrow hourglass stance)
15. Renoji-dachi (L-stance)
16. Neko-ashi-dachi (cat stance)

Try each stance in Figure 3.4 in front of a full-length mirror and compare it to the photograph of that stance.

Figure 3.4 Karate stances

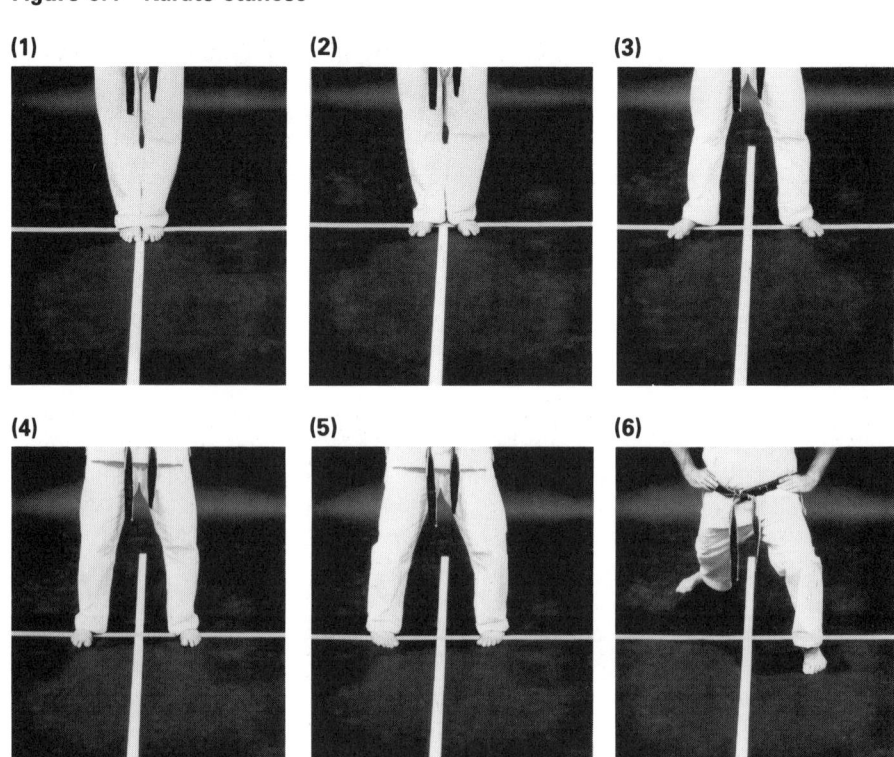

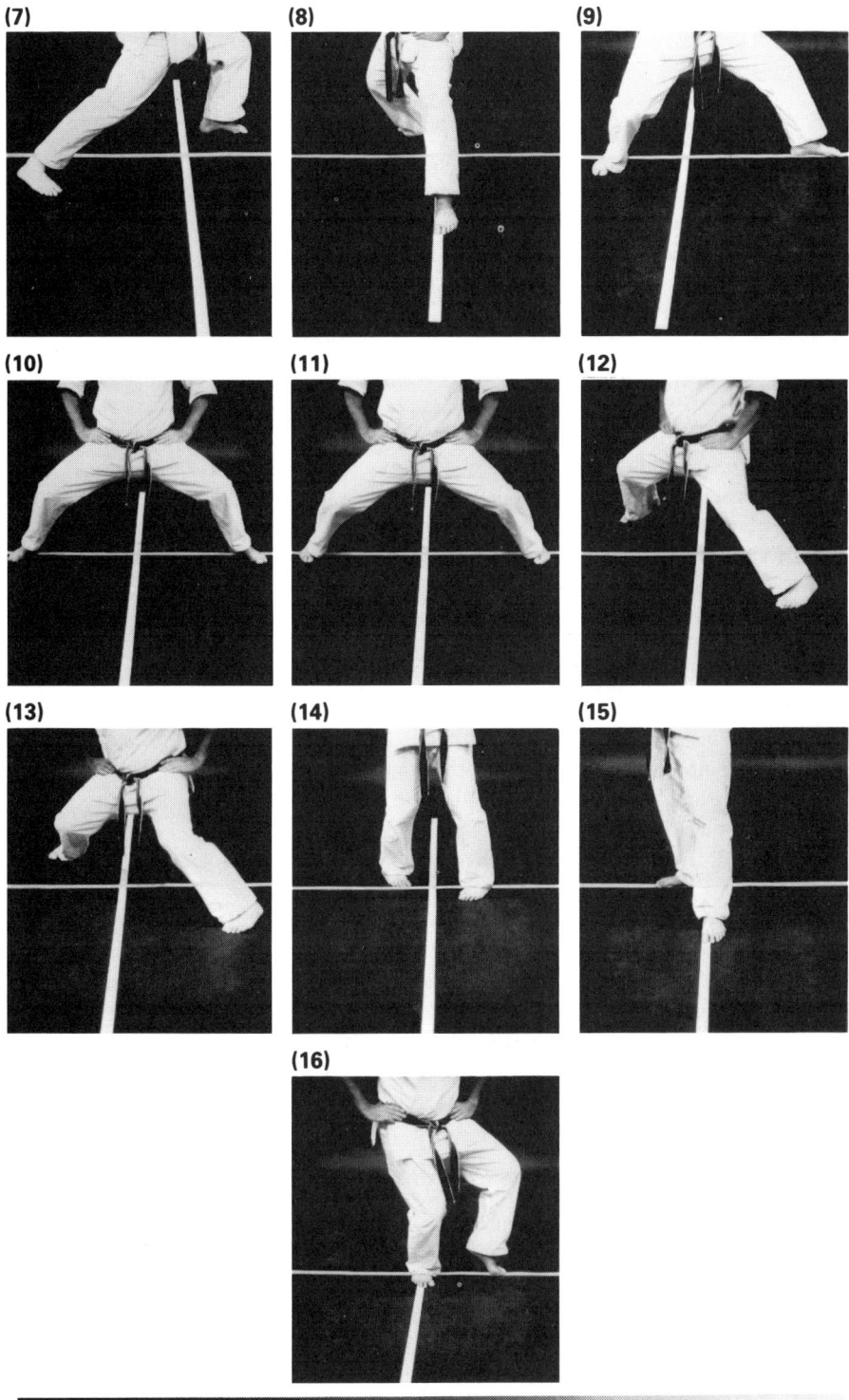

Kihon (Basic Techniques)

THE ERROR CORRECTOR

As you perform each stance in front of a full-length mirror identify and correct any body parts that are out of place until your stance looks like the one in the photograph. Repeat this often and try to memorize the feeling of each stance until you can move into any stance quickly and know that it is correct.

During all of these stances you should have your head up, your upper body erect, and your shoulders level. Do not lean with your upper body in your stances or during the performance of your karate techniques because it will put you off balance.

In karate there are four basic torso-facing positions: front-facing, half-front-facing, sideways-facing, and reverse-half-facing. The tremendous power that is generated in karate techniques is a result of efficient and coordinated use of the hips and shoulders. This is especially true during blocking and punching.

In the front-facing position, the torso, hips, and shoulders are facing directly forward and are perpendicular to the line of attack. The front-facing position is used during the bow, the ready position, and punching techniques.

In the half-front-facing position the torso, hips, and shoulders are positioned at a 45-degree angle to the line of attack. The half-front-facing position is frequently used during blocking techniques.

In the sideways-facing position the torso, hips, and shoulders are positioned sideways to your opponent and parallel to the line of attack. The sideways-facing position is generally used during free-fighting and body shifting practice as well as during some specific blocks, punches, strikes, and kicks.

In the reverse-half-facing position, the torso, hips, and shoulders are positioned sideways, but in a reversed fashion, to the line of attack. The reverse-half-facing position is used during some blocks, punches, and strikes.

BODY MOVEMENT

Stepping Forward and Backward from a Front Stance

From a right front stance bring your left foot, left leg, hips, and torso forward while keeping both feet as flat as possible. Step strongly and keep your hips and shoulders level. You should experience a feeling of strength in your right leg. Your stepping foot should be no higher than paper thickness off the floor. Near the completion of the stepping movement firmly extend, tense, and thrust rearward with your right leg. Briefly tense both legs and your hips for an instant. This will ensure a firm stable base from which to deliver strong techniques.

Now step forward from a left front stance to a right front stance in the same manner.

During the stepping sequence keep your center of gravity moving forward, also keep your hips and shoulders level. Do not let your hips sway from side to side.

When you step backward from one front stance to another front stance perform everything in the same manner, just reverse the sequence of movements.

This style of stepping is called "fumidashi." The supporting leg is extended strongly and the moving foot slides lightly over the floor.

There is another style of stepping called "fumikomi." The stepping foot is raised a few inches off the floor and brought down forcefully in a stomping fashion. This type of stepping is sometimes used to make a more forceful attack.

Figure 3.5 Stepping forward and backward from front stance

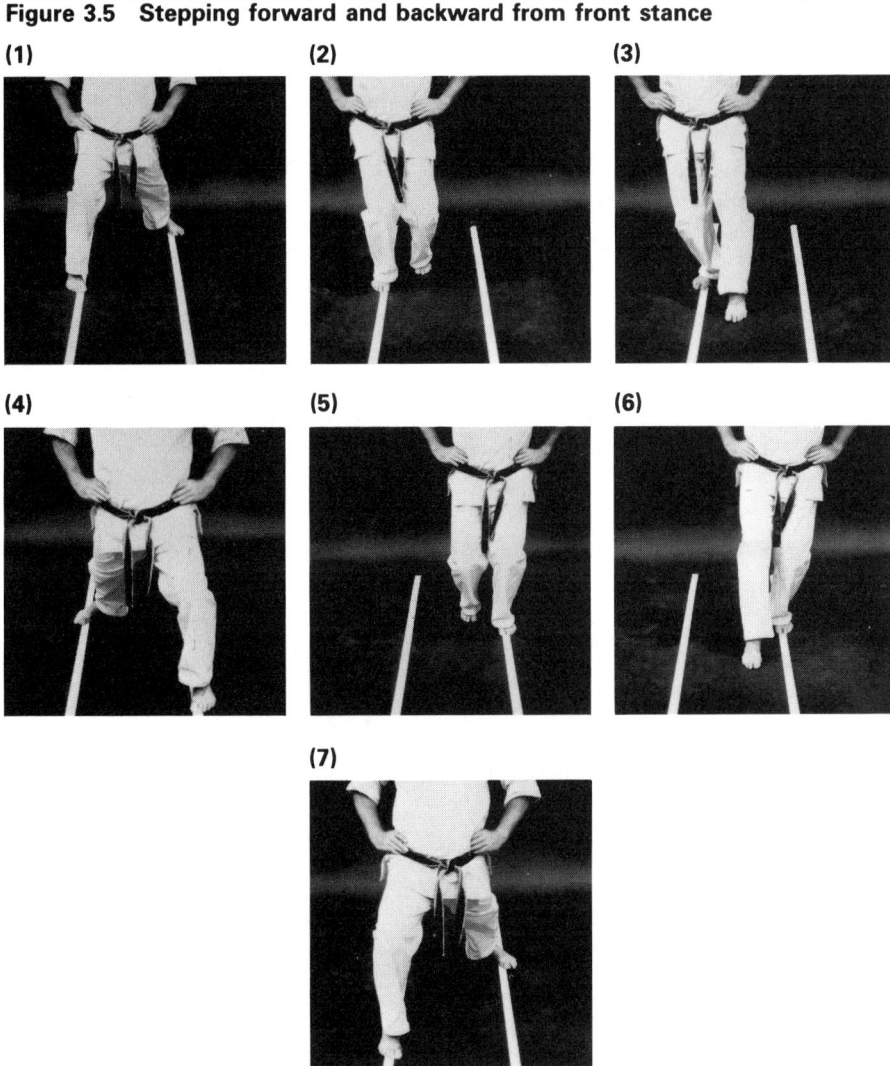

Kihon (Basic Techniques)

Stepping Forward and Backward from a Back Stance

Starting in a right back stance, slide your right foot forward until you are in a left back stance. As you complete the step tense both legs for an instant to give you a firm base from which you can perform powerful techniques. Keep your hips and shoulders level, also keep your center of gravity moving forward.

When stepping backward from a back stance, the method of moving is the same but the sequence of movements is reversed.

Figure 3.6 Stepping forward and backward from back stance

(1)

(2)

(3)

(4)

THE SPORT EXPERIENCE

1. Step forward from a front stance to a front stance.
2. Step backward from a front stance to a front stance.
3. Step forward from a back stance to a back stance.
4. Step backward from a back stance to a back stance.

THE ERROR CORRECTOR

After stepping forward and backward from a front stance and a back stance answer the following questions:

1. Did you keep both feet as flat as possible?
2. Did you keep your hips and shoulders level?
3. Did you step strongly and firmly?
4. Was your stepping foot kept very close to the floor? (It should not be lifted higher than the thickness of a piece of paper.)
5. Did you briefly tense both legs and hips for an instant when you arrived in a stance to form a stable base from which you could deliver a technique?
6. Did you keep your torso erect?
7. Did you keep your eyes focused straight to the front on your opponent or imaginary opponent?

Sliding Your Feet

"Yori-ashi" is a method of sliding both feet at the same time without changing your stance or posture. This can be done forward, backward, or to either side.

Another method of sliding your feet, "Tsugi-ashi" is performed when you step forward with your rear foot but stop before reaching the front foot, then step forward about the same distance with the front foot. In this manner you are able to move forward while keeping the same foot forward.

Reversing Direction

From a right front stance look over your left shoulder, move your left foot laterally about twice the width of your shoulders, and forcefully rotate your hips and shoulders to the left into a left front stance facing the opposite direction (see Figure 3.7). If a blocking, punching, or striking technique is executed during the turn the technique and the turn should finish at the same time. This turn can also be executed in the opposite direction, that is, from a left front stance to a right front stance. It may also be used to turn from other stances.

From a right front stance look over your right shoulder. Keeping your body erect step diagonally to the rear in a straight line, pivot on your left foot and finish in a right front stance facing the opposite direction (see Figure 3.8). Keep your hips and shoulders level throughout the turn. If a blocking, punching, or striking technique is executed during the turn the technique and the turn should finish at the same time. This turn can also be executed in the opposite direction, that is, from a left front stance to a left front stance. It may also be used to turn from other stances.

Figure 3.7 Reversing direction from right front stance (Method 1)   (1)   (2)

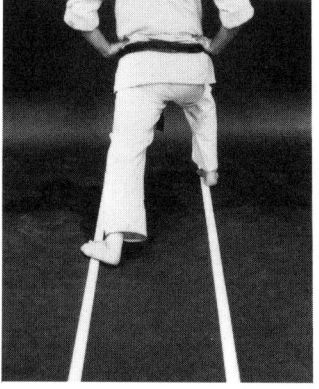 

Figure 3.8 Reversing direction from right front stance (Method 2)   (1)   (2)

THE SPORT EXPERIENCE

1. Perform a left 180-degree turn from a right front stance to a left front stance.
2. Perform a right 180-degree turn from a left front stance to a right front stance.
3. Perform a right 180-degree turn from a right front stance to right front stance.
4. Perform a left 180-degree turn from a left front stance to a left front stance.

THE ERROR CORRECTOR

After performing the 180-degree turns answer the following questions:

1. After doing a 180-degree turn to your left from a right front stance to a left front stance:
    a. Did you keep your torso erect?
    b. Did you look over your left shoulder before turning?
    c. Did you move your left foot laterally twice the width of your shoulders?
    d. Did you forcefully rotate your hips and shoulders as you made the turn?
    e. Did you finish in a stable left front stance facing the opposite direction?
2. After doing a 180-degree turn to your right from a left front stance to a right front stance:
    a. Did you keep your torso erect?
    b. Did you look over your right shoulder before turning?
    c. Did you move your right foot laterally twice the width of your shoulders?
    d. Did you forcefully rotate your hips and shoulders as you made the turn?
    e. Did you finish in a stable right front stance facing the opposite direction?

Kihon (Basic Techniques)

3. After doing a 180-degree turn to your right from a right front stance to a right front stance:
   a. Did you keep your torso erect?
   b. Did you look over your right shoulder before turning?
   c. Did you step diagonally to the rear in a straight line?
   d. Did you pivot on your left foot?
   e. Did you forcefully rotate your hips and shoulders as you made the turn?
   f. Did you finish in a stable right front stance facing the opposite direction?

4. After doing a 180-degree turn to your left from a left front stance to a left front stance:
   a. Did you keep your torso erect?
   b. Did you look over your left shoulder before turning?
   c. Did you step diagonally to the rear in a straight line?
   d. Did you pivot on your right foot?
   e. Did you forcefully rotate your hips and shoulders as you made the turn?
   f. Did you finish in a stable left front stance facing the opposite direction?

Body Shifting (Taisabaki)

"Taisabaki" refers to the ability to execute a body shifting movement so that you evade an opponent's attack and place yourself in position for an appropriate counterattack all in one movement. To become highly successful at this you must learn to use either foot as the pivot foot and be able to shift your position from any stance.

ATTACK AND DEFENSE LEVELS

In karate there are three levels of attack and defense: lower level (gedan), middle level (chūdan), and upper level (jōdan). Offensive and defensive techniques are aimed at one of these three areas.

The upper level (jōdan) covers the area between the top of the shoulders and the top of the head. The upper level blocks defend this area.

The middle level (chūdan) covers the area between the top of the shoulders and the solar plexus. The middle level blocks defend this area.

The lower level (gedan) covers the area starting just below the hips and extending upward to the solar plexus. The lower level blocks defend this area.

As you read through the next section of basic karate techniques try these Sport Experiences:

1. Study the sequence photographs, read the description of the technique, and try to perform each technique ten times.
2. Now try the techniques ten times to the opposite side.
3. Perform each technique in front of a full-length mirror and check for correct execution.
4. Have a karate training partner watch your technique for correct execution.
5. Videotape your performance of each technique and watch yourself for correct execution.
6. Perform one attack practice with a karate training partner. One of you performs a predetermined technique while the other one performs an appropriate countertechnique. For example, one of you performs a high level front lunge punch while the other one performs a high rising block. Be sure to agree about which technique will be used each time for safety during practice.
7. Perform three step sparring (sanbon kumite) in which one of you attacks three times in succession to the same target level using the same prearranged technique. The defender blocks each attack.
8. Perform five step sparring (gohon kumite) in which one of you attacks five consecutive times using the same attack each time directed at the same target level. The defender moves backward, blocking each attack.

BLOCKS

Down Block
(gedan barai)

Figure 3.9 (1) (2) (3)

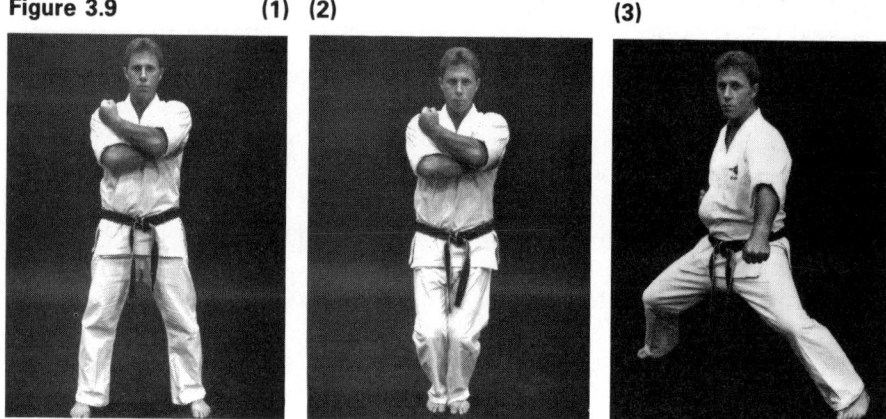

This block is used against a punch or kick that is directed toward your lower torso, abdominal area or lower.

From the yōi position, place your left fist near your right shoulder with the palm side toward your right ear. At the same time, place your right fist under your left armpit, palm down. Step back with your right foot to your right rear at a 45-degree angle into an immovable stance. Immediately execute a left down block as you turn your torso to a half-front-facing position and pull your right fist back to your right hip.

After performing the down block answer the following questions:

1. Was the down block effective in protecting against an attack directed at your lower torso area?
2. Did you move your foot in an arclike motion toward your opposite foot, then toward the rear?
3. Was your immovable stance correct and stable?
4. Did you keep your eyes focused to the front on your opponent?
5. Did you turn your torso forcefully to a half-front-facing position as you executed your block?
6. Did you forcefully pull your opposite fist to your hip as you executed your block?

Outside Forearm Chest Block, Inside Outward
(chūdan ude uke, uchi uke)

Figure 3.10   (1)   (2)   (3)

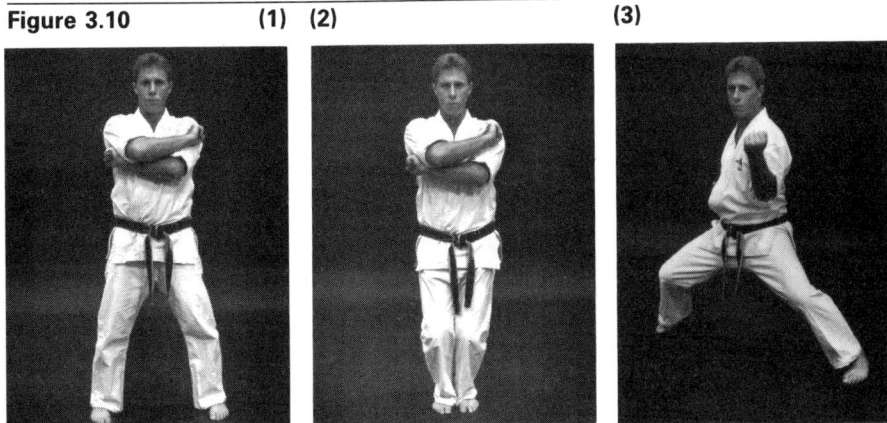

This block is used against a punch or kick aimed at your chest or face.

From the yōi position, cross your left arm under your right arm with the palm side of each fist facing away from your body. Step back with your right foot to your right rear at a 45-degree angle into an immovable stance. Immediately execute a left inside outward forearm chest block as you turn your torso to a half-front-facing position and pull your right fist back to your right hip.

After performing the outside forearm chest block answer the following questions:

1. Was the block effective in protecting the middle or chest level of your body?
2. Did you move your foot in an arclike motion toward your opposite foot, then toward the rear?
3. Was your immovable stance correct and stable?
4. Did you keep your eyes focused to the front on your opponent?
5. Did you turn your torso forcefully to a half-front-facing position as you executed your block?
6. Did you forcefully pull your opposite fist to your hip as you executed your block?

Knife Hand Block
(shūtō uke)

Figure 3.11   **(1)**   **(2)**   **(3)**

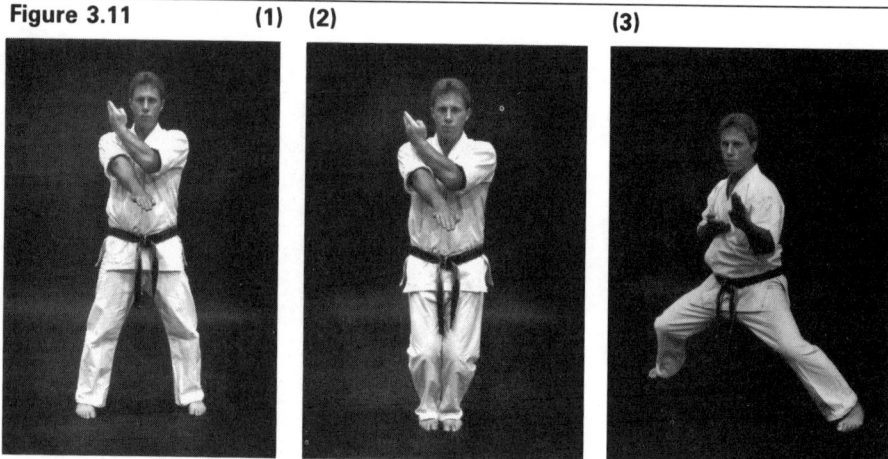

This block is used against an attack aimed at your upper abdomen, chest, or face.

From the yōi position, place your left open hand near your right shoulder with the palm toward your right ear. With your right arm fully extended, place your right open hand in front of your body, palm down and waist high. Step back with your right foot to your right rear at a 45-degree angle into an immovable stance. Immediately execute a middle level knife hand block with your left hand as you turn your torso to a half-front-facing position and pull your right hand to your solar plexus with the palm facing upward.

After performing the knife hand block answer the following questions:

1. Was the block effective in protecting you from a middle level attack?
2. Did you move your foot in an arclike motion toward your opposite foot, then toward the rear?
3. Was your immovable stance correct and stable?
4. Did you keep your eyes focused to the front on your opponent?
5. Did you turn your torso forcefully to a half-front-facing position as you executed your block?
6. Did you pull your opposite hand to your solar plexus with the palm facing upward?

High Open Hand Catching Block
(jōdan sukui uke)

Figure 3.12   (1) (2)   (3)

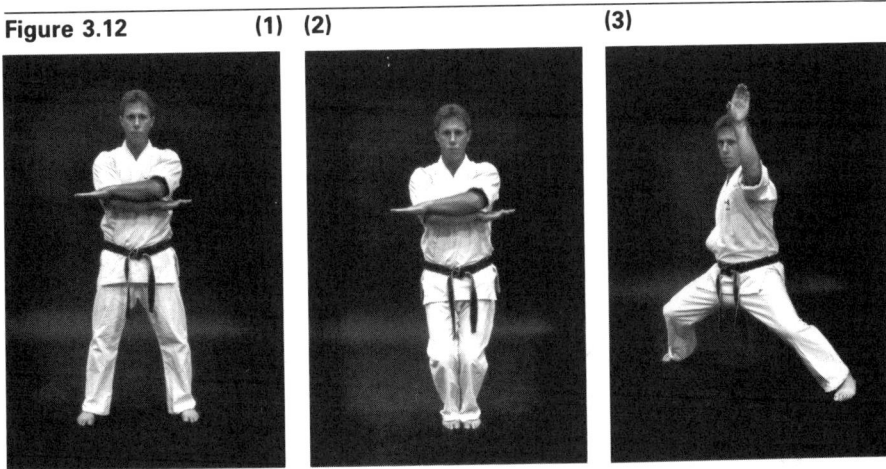

This block is used against a punch or kick that is aimed at your face.

From the yōi position, place your left forearm over your right forearm with both open palms facing down. Step back with your right foot to your right rear at a 45-degree angle into an immovable stance. Immediately execute a high left open hand catching block as you turn your torso to a half-front-facing position and pull your right fist back to your right hip.

After performing the high open hand catching block answer the following questions:

1. Was the block effective in protecting you from a high level or face attack?
2. Did you move your foot in an arclike motion toward your opposite foot, then toward the rear?
3. Was your immovable stance correct and stable?
4. Did you keep your eyes focused to the front on your opponent?
5. Did you turn your torso forcefully to a half-front-facing position as you executed your block?
6. Did you forcefully pull your opposite fist to your hip as you executed your block?

Kihon (Basic Techniques)

Rising High Block
(jōdan age uke)

Figure 3.13 (1) (2) (3)

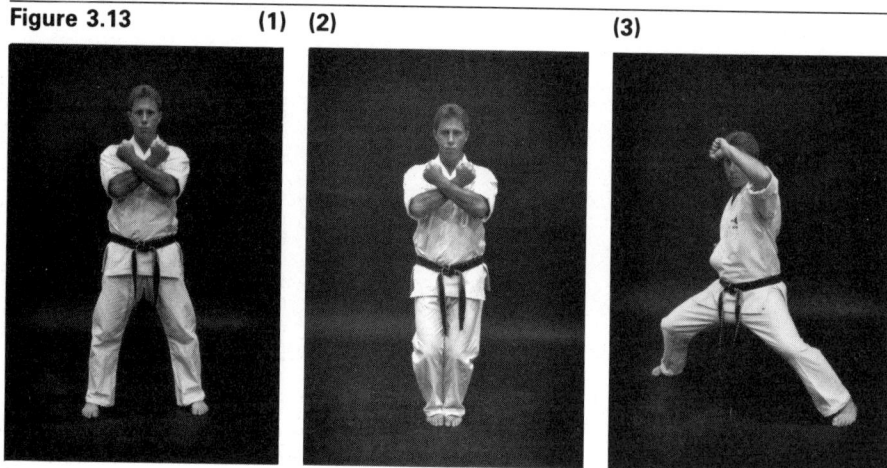

This block is used against an attack that is directed toward your upper chest or face.

From the yōi position, form an X with your forearms in front of your chest, left in front of right, with the palms of both fists facing your body. Step back with your right foot to your right rear at a 45-degree angle into an immovable stance. Execute a left rising high block as you turn your torso to a half-front-facing position and pull your right fist back to your right hip.

After performing the rising high block answer the following questions:

1. Was the block effective in protecting you from a high level or face attack?
2. Did you move your foot in an arclike motion toward your opposite foot, then toward the rear?
3. Was your immovable stance correct and stable?
4. Did you keep your eyes focused to the front on your opponent?
5. Did you turn your torso forcefully to a half-front-facing position as you executed your block?
6. Did you forcefully pull your opposite fist to your hip as you executed your block?

High Forearm Block, Outside Inward
(jōdan soto ude uke)

Figure 3.14 (1) (2) (3)

This block is used against a punch or kick aimed at your upper chest or face.

From the yōi position, keep your right arm straight and place your right fist in front of your body at mid-chest level. With your left elbow at a 90-degree angle, place your left arm to the side of your body at shoulder level so that your left upper arm is horizontal and your left forearm is perpendicular. Step back with your right foot to your right rear at a 45-degree angle into an immovable stance. Immediately execute a left outside inward high forearm block as you turn to a half-front-facing position and pull your right fist back to your right hip.

THE ERROR CORRECTOR

After performing the high forearm block from outside inward answer the following questions:

1. Was the block effective in protecting you from a high level or face attack?
2. Did you move your foot in an arclike motion toward your opposite foot, then toward the rear?
3. Was your immovable stance correct and stable?
4. Did you keep your eyes focused to the front on your opponent?
5. Did you turn your torso forcefully to a half-front-facing position as you executed your block?
6. Did you forcefully pull your opposite fist to your hip as you executed your block?

PUNCHES

Middle Level Lunge Punch
(chūdan oi zuki)

Figure 3.15   (1)   (2)   (3)

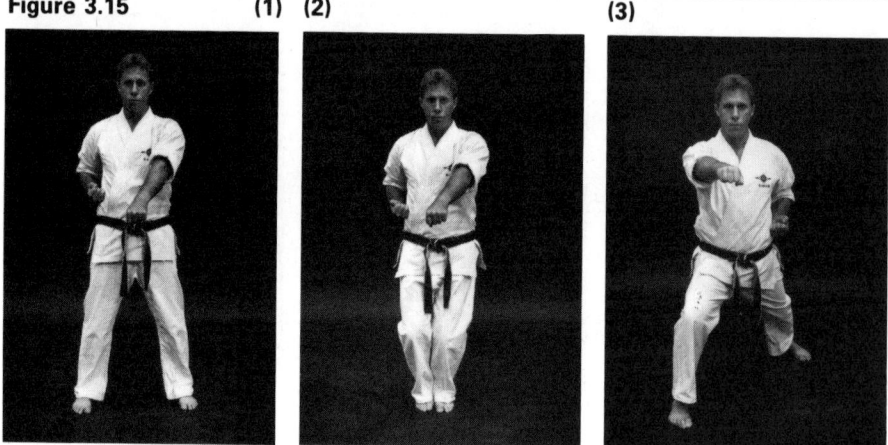

From the yōi position, leave your left fist in place and pull your right fist to your right hip, palm up. Slide your right foot next to your left foot, then forward into a right front stance while punching with your right fist to the middle chest position and pulling your left fist back to your left hip, palm up. Your right fist should remain palm up until the moment of impact, then it should rotate.

After performing the middle level lunge punch answer the following questions:

1. Was your punch delivered forcefully?
2. Did your punching fist remain in a palm up position until impact?
3. Did you pull your opposite fist forcefully to the rear as you delivered your punch?
4. Did you keep your torso erect?
5. Did you keep your shoulders from rotating?
6. Did you avoid leaning into the punch?
7. Did you move your foot in an arclike motion toward the other foot, then forward into a front stance?
8. Was your front stance correct and stable?

High Level Lunge Punch
(jōdan oi zuki)

Figure 3.16

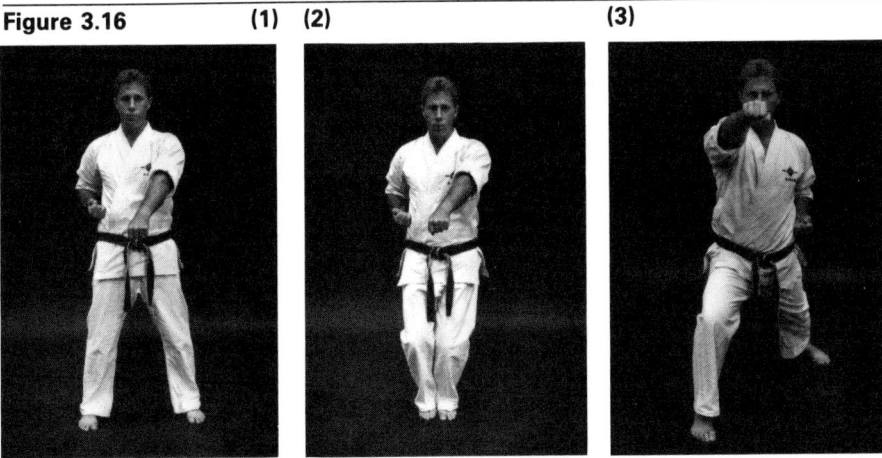

From the yōi position, leave your left fist in place and pull your right fist to your right hip, palm up. Slide your right foot next to your left foot, then forward into a right front stance while punching with your right fist to the face and pulling your left fist back to your left hip, palm up. Your right fist should remain palm up until the moment of impact, then it should rotate.

THE ERROR CORRECTOR

After performing the high level lunge punch answer the following questions:

1. Was your punch delivered forcefully?
2. Did your punching fist remain in a palm up position until impact?
3. Did you pull your opposite fist forcefully to the rear as you delivered your punch?
4. Did you keep your torso erect?
5. Did you keep your shoulders from rotating?
6. Did you avoid leaning into the punch?
7. Did you move your foot in an arclike motion toward the other foot, then forward into a front stance?
8. Was your front stance correct and stable?

Kihon (Basic Techniques)

Middle Level Reverse Punch
(chūdan gyaku zuki)

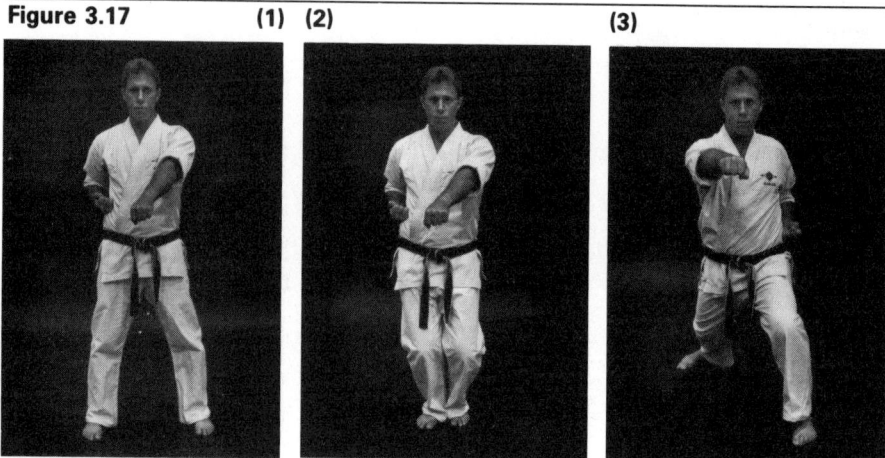

Figure 3.17 (1) (2) (3)

From the yōi position, leave your left fist in place and pull your right fist to your right hip, palm up. Slide your left foot next to your right foot, then forward into a left front stance while punching with your right fist to the middle chest position and pulling your left fist back to your left hip, palm up. Your right fist should remain palm up until the moment of impact, then it should rotate.

THE ERROR CORRECTOR

After performing the middle level reverse punch answer the following questions:

1. Was your punch delivered forcefully?
2. Did your punching fist remain in a palm up position until impact?
3. Did you pull your opposite fist forcefully to the rear as you delivered your punch?
4. Did you keep your torso erect?
5. Did you keep your shoulders from rotating?
6. Did you avoid leaning into the punch?
7. Did you move your foot in an arclike motion toward the other foot, then forward into a front stance?
8. Was your front stance correct and stable?

High Level Reverse Punch
(jōdan gyaku zuki)

Figure 3.18   **(1)**   **(2)**   **(3)**

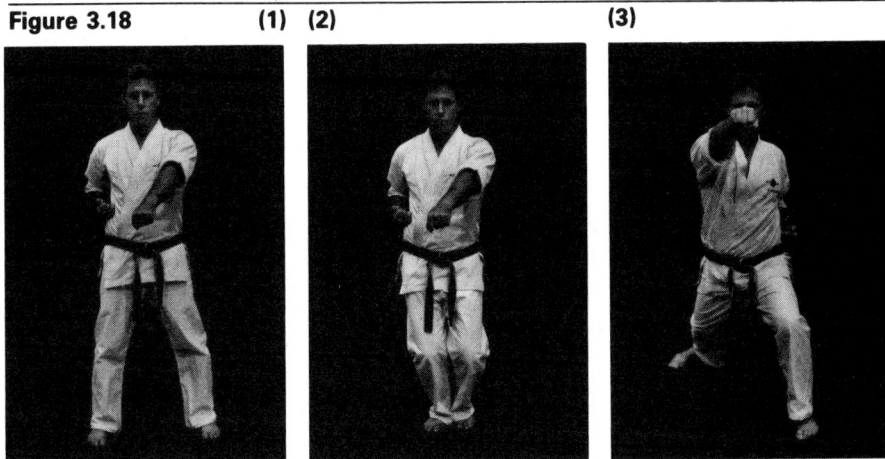

From the yōi position, leave your left fist in place and pull your right fist to your right hip, palm up. Slide your left foot next to your right foot, then forward into a left front stance while punching with your right fist to the face and pulling your left fist back to your left hip, palm up. Your right fist should remain palm up until the moment of impact, then it should rotate.

THE ERROR CORRECTOR

After performing the high level reverse punch answer the following questions:

1. Was your punch delivered forcefully?
2. Did your punching fist remain in a palm up position until impact?
3. Did you pull your opposite fist forcefully to the rear as you delivered your punch?
4. Did you keep your torso erect?
5. Did you keep your shoulders from rotating?
6. Did you avoid leaning into the punch?
7. Did you move your foot in an arclike motion toward the other foot, then forward into a front stance?
8. Was your front stance correct and stable?

KICKS

Front Kick
(mae geri)

Figure 3.19

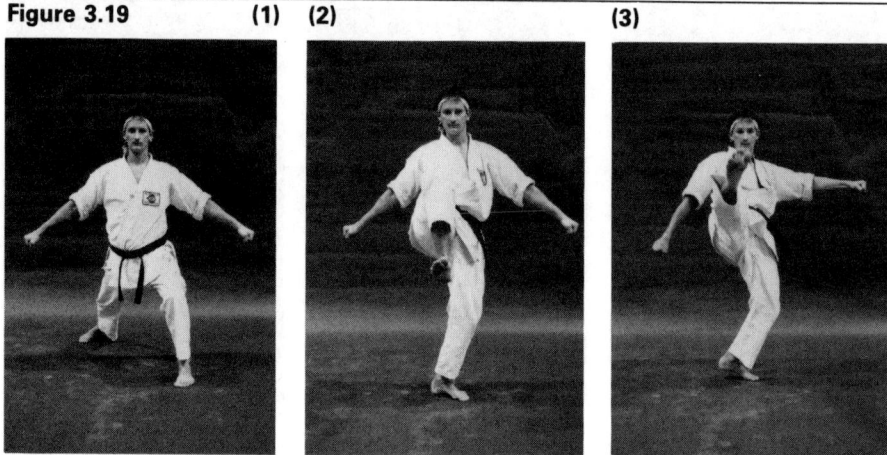

From a left front stance, raise your right knee as high and as close to your chest as possible while keeping your torso erect. Extend your hip and right leg forcefully toward your target. Keep your toes pulled up so that you strike your target with the ball of your right foot. Your left leg should remain slightly bent at the knee.

After performing the front kick answer the following questions:
1. Was your kick delivered forcefully?
2. Was your kick delivered accurately?
3. Did you bring the knee of your kicking leg as high and as close to your chest as possible?
4. Did you keep your toes pulled up so that you could strike with the ball of your foot?
5. Did you keep your torso erect as you brought your knee up toward your chest?
6. Did you keep your supporting foot in a stable position on the floor?

Round Kick
(mawashi geri)

Figure 3.20 (1) (2) (3)

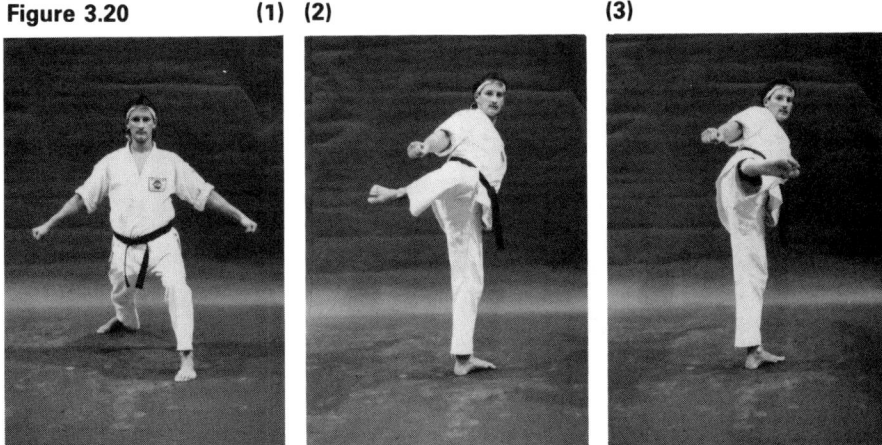

From a left front stance, raise your right knee as high as possible in front of your chest while keeping your torso erect. Pivot on your left foot and rotate your kicking leg to a horizontal position. Extend your kicking leg forcefully and strike your target with the ball of your foot or with the instep. Your support leg should remain slightly bent at the knee and your support foot should be flat on the floor.

After performing the round kick answer the following questions:

1. Was your kick delivered forcefully?
2. Was your kick delivered accurately?
3. Did you pivot on your supporting foot?
4. Did you rotate your kicking leg to a horizontal position before kicking?
5. Did you keep your toes pulled up so that you could strike with the ball of your foot?
6. Did you keep your torso erect as you brought your knee up?
7. Did you keep your supporting foot in a stable position on the floor?

Kihon (Basic Techniques)

Side Kick
(yoko geri)

Figure 3.21

From a straddle stance, look to your left and bring your right foot in front of your left foot. With your weight on your right foot and your right knee slightly bent, bring your left knee as high and as close to your chest as possible while keeping your torso erect. As you extend your hip and kicking leg forcefully to your left allow your torso to bend and counterbalance naturally. Strike your target with the outside edge of your foot or your heel.

After performing the side kick answer the following questions:

1. Did you look to the side at your opponent before moving in that direction?
2. Did you bring the knee of your kicking leg as high and as close to your chest as possible?
3. Did you keep your torso erect as you brought your knee up?
4. Did you deliver your kick forcefully?
5. Did you deliver your kick accurately?

Back Kick
(ushiro geri)

Figure 3.22 (1) (2) (3) (4)

From a straddle stance, look to your left and bring your right foot behind your left foot. With your weight on your right foot and your right knee slightly bent bring your left knee toward your chest while keeping your torso erect. As you extend your hip and kicking leg forcefully to the rear allow your upper body to bend and counterbalance naturally. Strike your target with your heel.

After performing the back kick answer the following questions:

1. Did you look to the rear at your opponent before moving in that direction?
2. Did you keep your torso erect as you brought your knee up?
3. Did you keep your eyes on your opponent at all times?
4. Did you keep your support foot flat on the floor?
5. Was your kick forceful?
6. Was your kick accurate?

Kata (Formal Exercises)

The movements that you learn in kihon (basic techniques) are practiced in kata (formal exercises) and are applied in kumite (sparring). In a kata the basic techniques of blocking, punching, striking, and kicking are arranged in a formal sequence that is performed against imaginary opponents. There are a fixed number of movements in a kata and they must be performed in the correct order.

Since a kata is composed of basic techniques, it would seem rather simple to learn. However, the correct performance of a kata requires years of practice. The performer must become one with the kata and bring the kata to life, much as an actor brings a character to life or a dancer brings a dance to life. This requires careful attention to every detail in order to obtain the correct power, speed, rhythm, timing, and meaning.

There is a predetermined performance line (embusen) to follow for each kata. The shape of this performance line is not the same for every kata. The first movement and the last movement of each kata are generally performed at the same point on the performance line. It is proper to bow at the beginning and at the end of a kata.

The speed of movement varies within each kata. In addition to this, some kata are slower than others. The slower kata are primarily used to develop strength while the faster kata are primarily used to develop speed. Each kata contains movements that exercise the entire body. Repetitious practice of the kata will result in defense and counterattack sequences that are automatic. These sequences will be very fast compared to movements that require thought and planning.

Everyone who participates in karate needs kata practice, regardless of rank or skill level. Kata practice may be performed alone or in a group.

TEN-NO-KATA
(Kata of the Universe)

The techniques in Ten-No-Kata form the foundation of one-step prearranged sparring. This kata consists of four attack techniques, executed to the front of a stationary point on the floor, and six techniques of defense and counterattack, executed to the rear of a stationary point on the floor.

Each of the ten techniques is executed four times in an alternating sequence of right, left, right, left.

To gain the maximum benefit from kata practice you must imagine defending yourself, and attacking an opponent. Always be sincere about this in your training.

Each technique should be executed with good form, with maximum force, and with focus. Your eyes and mind should always be focused straight ahead on the imagined opponent.

Begin the kata with a bow (rei). After you bow assume the ready position (yōi). Slowly return to the yōi position after the execution of each technique. With the performance of the last (fourth) attack in each technique sequence there should be a "kiai" (spirit cry or karate shout). End the kata with a bow.

Ten-No-Kata Embusen

The Ten-No-Kata embusen (performance line) consists of taking one step to the front of a stationary point during each of the four attack techniques and one step to the rear of a stationary point during each of the defense and counterattack sequences. Each step is taken in an arclike motion. After each technique is performed, slowly return to the yōi position moving your foot in an arclike motion. Figure 4.1 illustrates these techniques.

Figure 4.1 Ten-No-Kata

Embusen (performance line or stepping sequence)

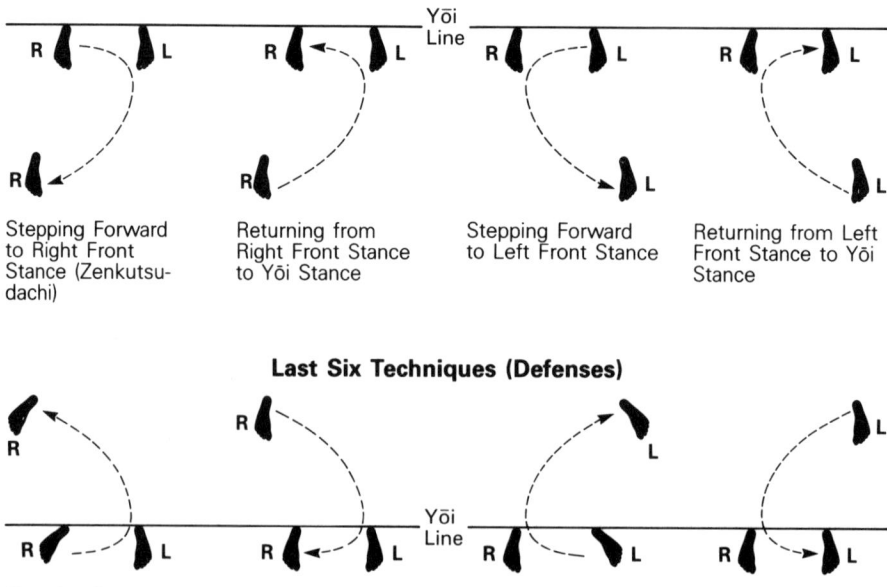

This Sport Experience is for the first kata, Ten-No-Kata.

1. Study the sequence photographs, read the technique description, and perform each technique four times in an alternating sequence of right, left, right, left.
2. Perform each technique in front of a full-length mirror to check for correct execution.
3. Videotape your performance so that you can study yourself performing these techniques.
4. Practice one technique at a time until you are comfortable with each of them.
5. Perform the first technique followed by the second technique. Continue to add one technique at a time until you can perform the whole kata.

Ten-No-Kata Technique Number 1

Technique: Middle Level Lunge Punch (chūdan oizuki)

Stance: Front Stance (zenkutsu-dachi)

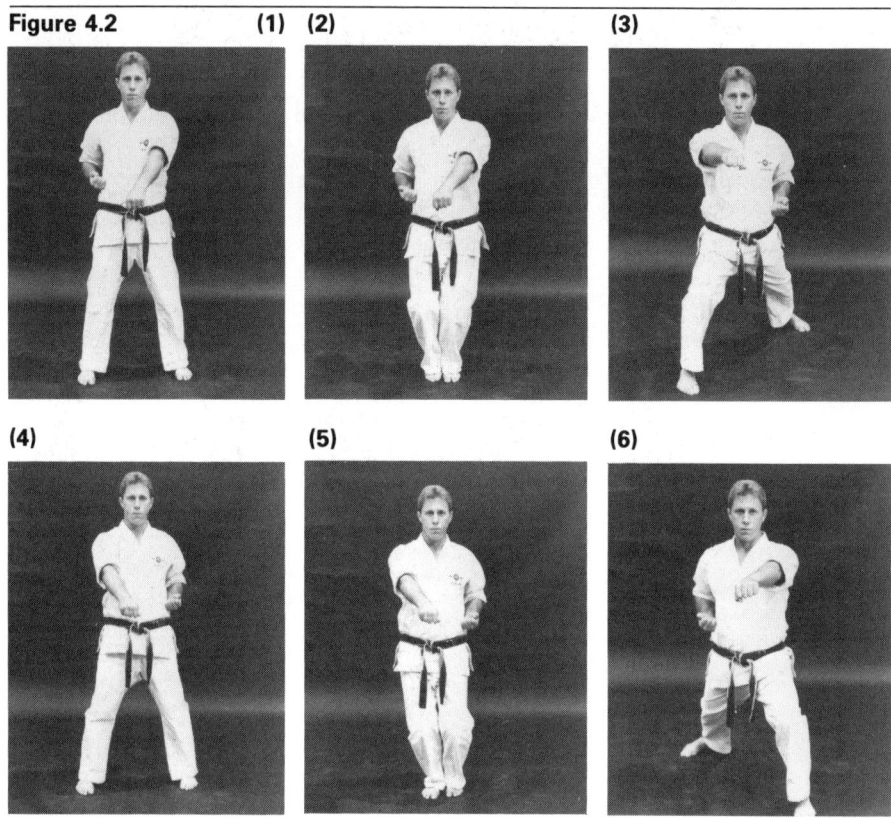

Figure 4.2

Leave your left fist in the yōi position. Pull your right fist to your right hip, palm up. **(1)**

Step forward with your right foot into a right front stance while pulling your left fist back to your left hip (palm up) **(2)** and punching with your right fist to the middle chest position. **(3)**

Your right fist should remain palm up until the moment of imagined contact, then it should rotate on impact. Return to the starting position.

Leave your right fist in the yōi position. Pull your left fist to your left hip, palm up. **(4)**

Step forward with your left foot into a left front stance while pulling your right fist back to your right hip (palm up) **(5)** and punching with your left fist to the middle chest position. **(6)**

Your left fist should remain palm up until the moment of imagined contact, then it should rotate on impact. Return to the starting position.

Ten-No-Kata Technique Number 2

Technique: High Level Lunge Punch (jōdan oizuki)

Stance: Front Stance (zenkutsu-dachi)

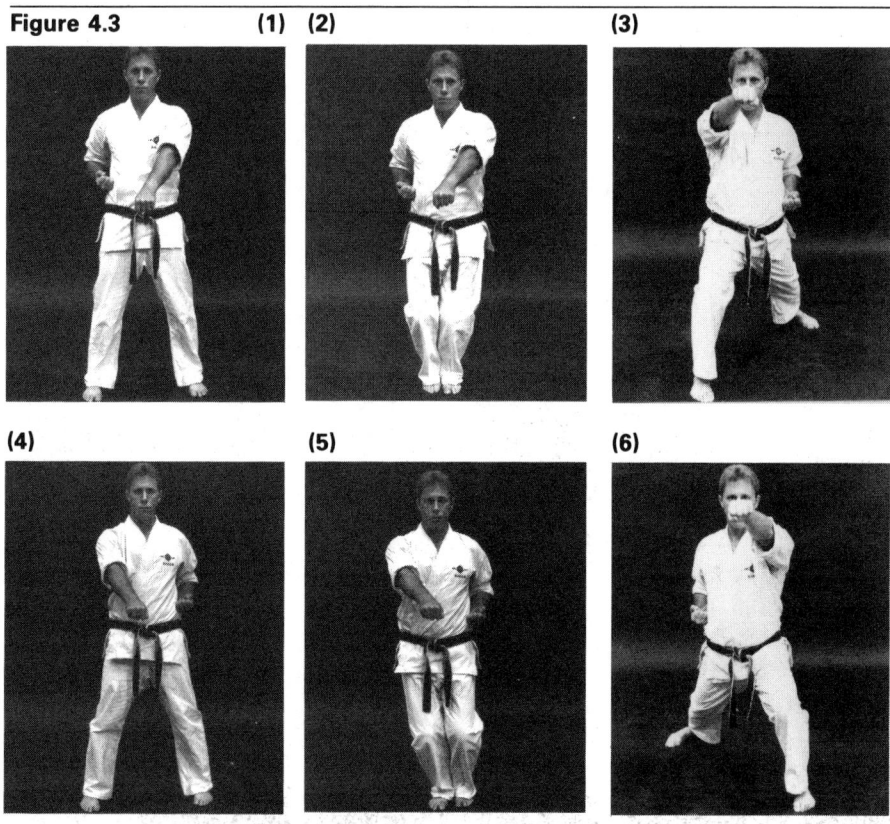

Figure 4.3

Leave your left fist in the yōi position. Pull your right fist to your right hip, palm up. **(1)**

Step forward with your right foot into a front stance while pulling your left fist back to your left hip (palm up) **(2)** and punching with your right fist to the face level. **(3)**

Your right fist should remain palm up until the moment of imagined contact, then it should rotate on impact. Return to the starting position.

Leave your right fist in the yōi position. Pull your left fist to your left hip, palm up. **(4)**

Step forward with your left foot into a left front stance while pulling your right fist back to your right hip (palm up) **(5)** and punching with your left fist to the face level. **(6)**

Your left fist should remain palm up until the moment of imagined contact, then it should rotate on impact. Return to the starting position.

Ten-No-Kata Technique Number 3

Technique: Middle Level Reverse Punch (chūdan gyaku-zuki)

Stance: Front Stance (zenkutsu-dachi)

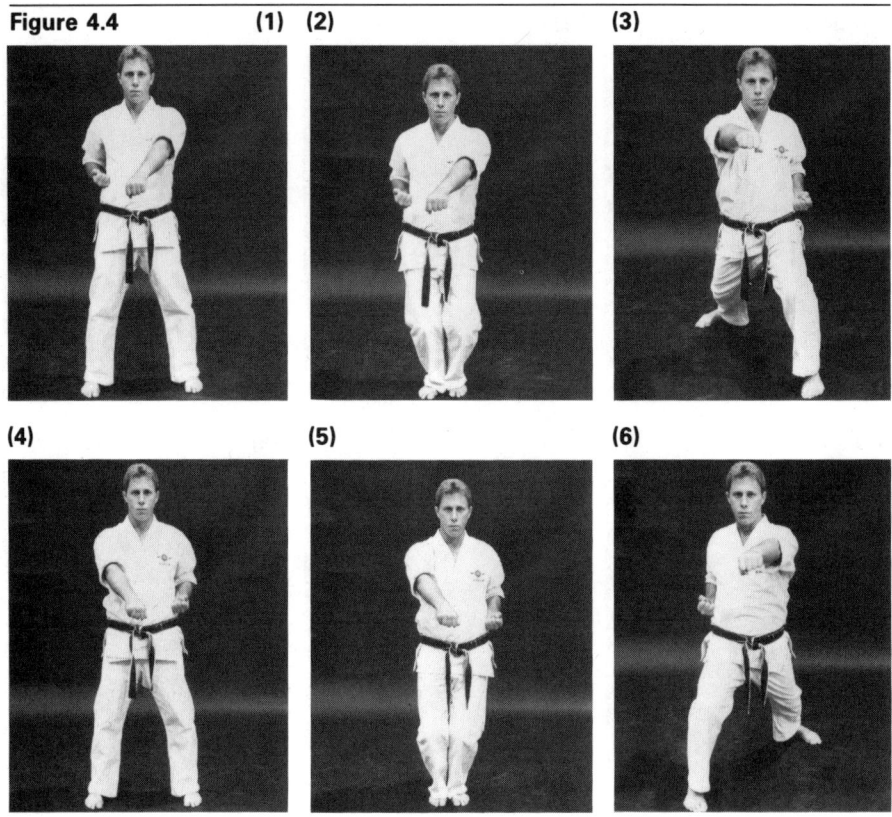

Figure 4.4

Leave your left fist in the yōi position. Pull your right fist to your right hip, palm up. **(1)**

Step forward with your left foot into a left front stance while pulling your left fist back to your left hip (palm up) **(2)** and punching with your right fist to the middle chest position. **(3)**

Your right fist should remain palm up until the moment of imagined contact, then it should rotate on impact. Return to the starting position.

Leave your right fist in the yōi position. Pull your left fist to your left hip, palm up. **(4)**

Step forward with your right foot into a right front stance while pulling your right fist back to your right hip (palm up) **(5)** and punching with your left fist to the middle chest position. **(6)**

Your left fist should remain palm up until the moment of imagined contact, then it should rotate on impact. Return to the starting position.

Ten-No-Kata Technique Number 4

Technique: High Level Reverse Punch (jōdan gyaku-zuki)

Stance: Front Stance (zenkutsu-dachi)

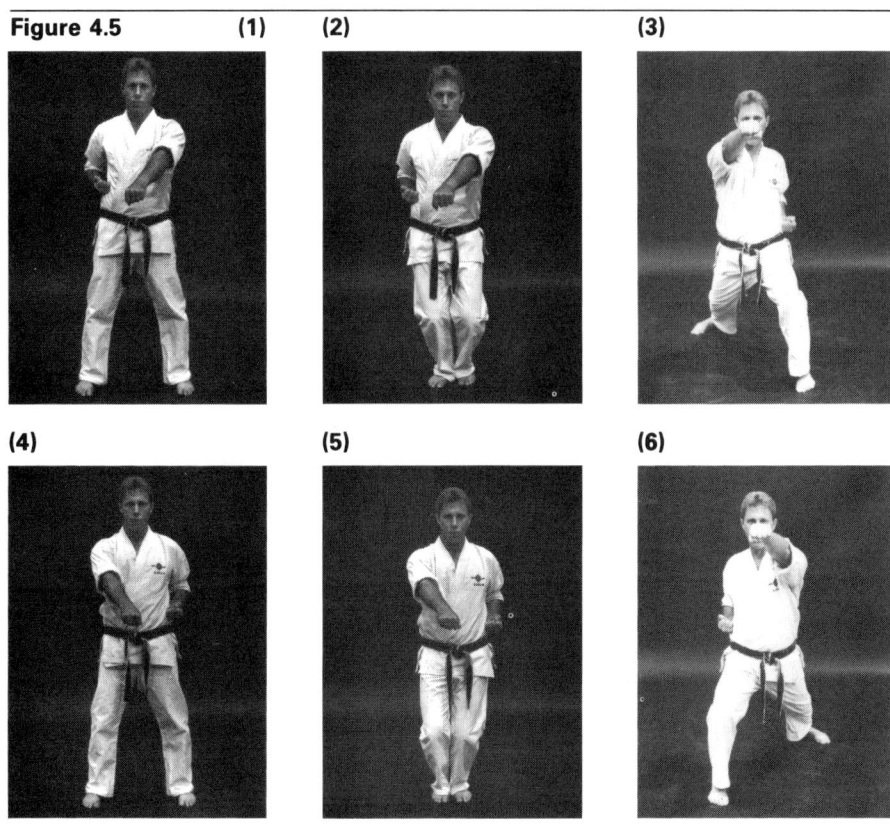

Figure 4.5

Leave your left fist in the yōi position. Pull your right fist to your right hip, palm up. **(1)**

Step forward with your left foot into a left front stance while pulling your left fist back to your left hip (palm up) **(2)** and punching with your right fist to the face level. **(3)**

Your right fist should remain palm up until the moment of imagined contact, then it should rotate on impact. Return to the starting position.

Leave your right fist in the yōi position. Pull your left fist to your left hip, palm up. **(4)**

Step forward with your right foot into a right front stance while pulling your right fist back to your right hip (palm up) **(5)** and punching with your left fist to the face level. **(6)**

Your left fist should remain palm up until the moment of imagined contact, then it should rotate on impact. Return to the starting position.

Ten-No-Kata Technique Number 5

Technique: Down Block/Middle Level Reverse Punch (gedan-barai/chūdan gyaku-zuki)

Stance: Immovable Stance (fudō-dachi)

Figure 4.6

Place your left fist near your right shoulder with the palm side toward your right ear. At the same time place your right fist under your left armpit, palm down. **(1)**

Step back with your right foot to your right rear at a 45-degree angle into an immovable stance. **(2)** Immediately execute a left down block with your torso in a half-front-facing position. **(3)**

Rotate your shoulders as you execute a middle level reverse punch. **(4)** Return to the starting position.

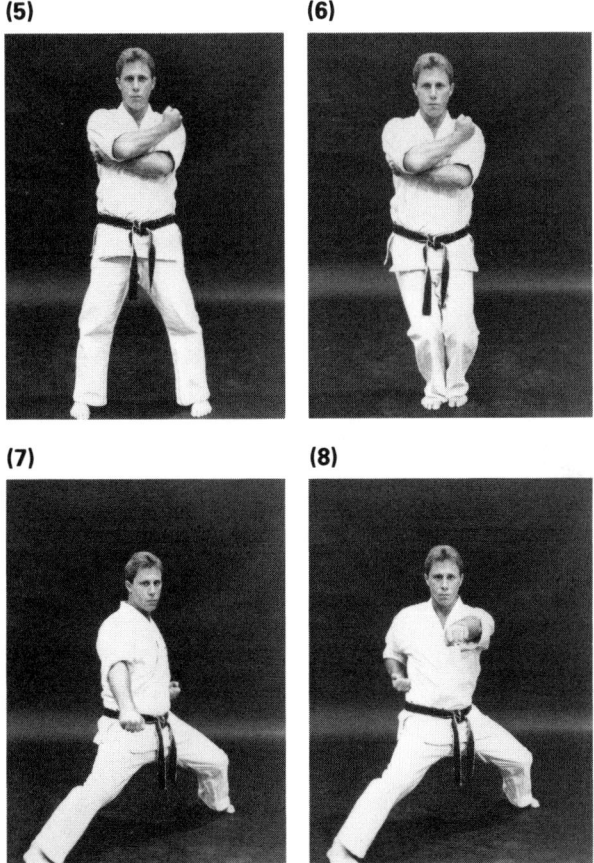

Place your right fist near your left shoulder with the palm side toward your left ear. At the same time place your left fist under your right armpit, palm down. **(5)**

Step back with your left foot to your left rear at a 45-degree angle into an immovable stance. **(6)** Immediately execute a right down block with your torso in a half-front-facing position. **(7)**

Rotate your shoulders as you execute a middle level reverse punch. **(8)** Return to the starting position.

Ten-No-Kata Technique Number 6

Technique: Center Block/Middle Level Reverse Punch (chūdan-uke/chūdan gyaku-zuki)

Stance: Immovable Stance (fudō-dachi)

Figure 4.7

Cross your left arm under your right arm. The palm side of each fist should be facing away from your body. **(1)**

Step back with your right foot to your right rear at a 45-degree angle into an immovable stance. **(2)** Immediately execute a left inside forearm chest block with your torso in a half-front-facing position. **(3)**

Rotate your shoulders as you execute a middle level reverse punch. **(4)** Return to the starting position.

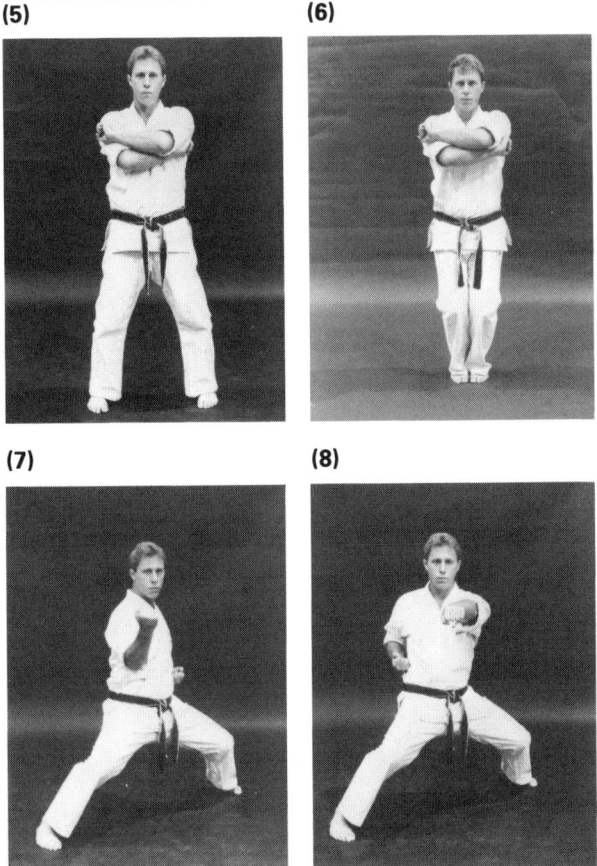

Cross your right arm under your left arm. The palm side of each fist should be facing away from your body. **(5)**

Step back with your left foot to your left rear at a 45-degree angle into an immovable stance. **(6)** Immediately execute a right inside forearm chest block with your torso in a half-front-facing position. **(7)**

Rotate your shoulders as you execute a middle level reverse punch. **(8)** Return to the starting position.

Ten-No-Kata Technique Number 7

Technique: Knife Hand Block (shūtō-uke)
Center Spear Hand Thrust (chūdan nukite)

Stance: Immovable Stance (fudō-dachi)

Figure 4.8

Place your left open hand near your right shoulder with the palm toward your right ear. With your right arm fully extended, place your right open hand in front of your body, palm down and waist high. **(1)**

Step back with your right foot to your right rear at a 45-degree angle into an immovable stance. **(2)** Immediately execute a middle level knife hand block. **(3)**

Rotate your shoulders as your execute a middle level spear hand thrust. **(4)** Return to the starting position.

Place your right open hand near your left shoulder with the palm toward your left ear. With your left arm fully extended, place your left open hand in front of your body, palm down and waist high. **(5)**

Step back with your left foot to your left rear at a 45-degree angle into an immovable stance. **(6)** Immediately execute a middle level knife hand block. **(7)**

Rotate your shoulders as you execute a middle level spear hand thrust. **(8)** Return to the starting position.

Kata (Formal Exercises)

Ten-No-Kata Technique Number 8

Technique: High Open Hand Catching Block (jōdan sukui-uke)
High Level Reverse Punch (jōdan gyaku-zuki)

Stance: Immovable Stance (fudō-dachi)

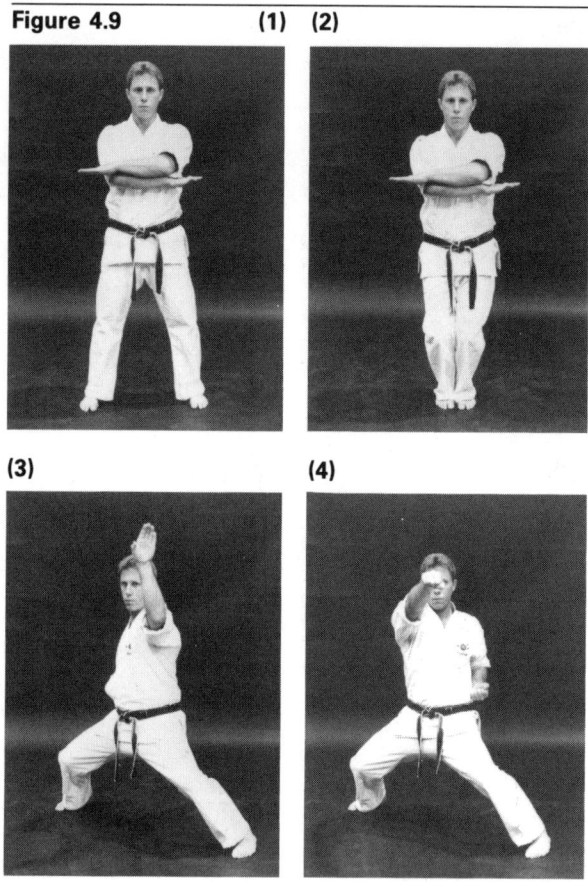

Figure 4.9

Place your left forearm over your right forearm with both open palms facing down. **(1)**

Step back with your right foot to your right rear at a 45-degree angle into an immovable stance. **(2)** Immediately execute a high left open hand catching block with your torso in a half-front-facing position and your right fist on your right hip. **(3)**

Rotate your shoulders as you execute a face level reverse punch with your right fist. **(4)** Return to the starting position.

Place your right forearm over your left forearm with both palms facing down. **(5)** Step back with your left foot to your left rear at a 45-degree angle into an immovable stance. **(6)** Immediately execute a high right open hand catching block with your torso in a half-front-facing position and your left fist on your left hip. **(7)** Rotate your shoulders as you execute a face level reverse punch with your left fist. **(8)** Return to the starting position.

Ten-No-Kata Technique Number 9

Technique: Rising High Block (jōdan-uke)
Middle Level Reverse Punch (chūdan gyaku-zuki)

Stance: Immovable Stance (fudō-dachi)

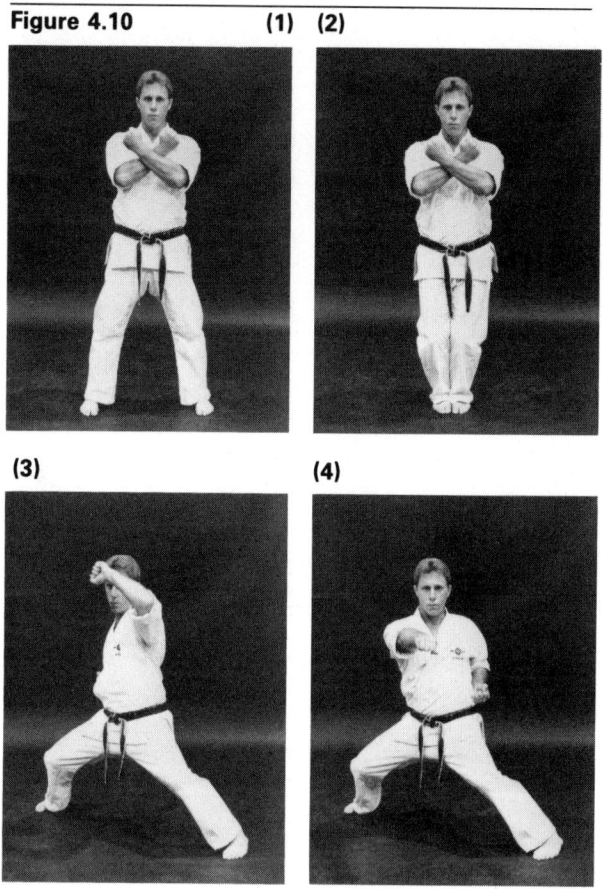

Figure 4.10

Form an X with your forearms in front of your chest, left in front of right, with the palms of both fists facing your body. **(1)**

Step back with your right foot to your right rear at a 45-degree angle into an immovable stance. **(2)** Execute a left rising high block with your torso in a half-front-facing position and your right fist on your right hip. **(3)**

Rotate your shoulders as your execute a middle level reverse punch with your right hand. **(4)** Return to the starting position.

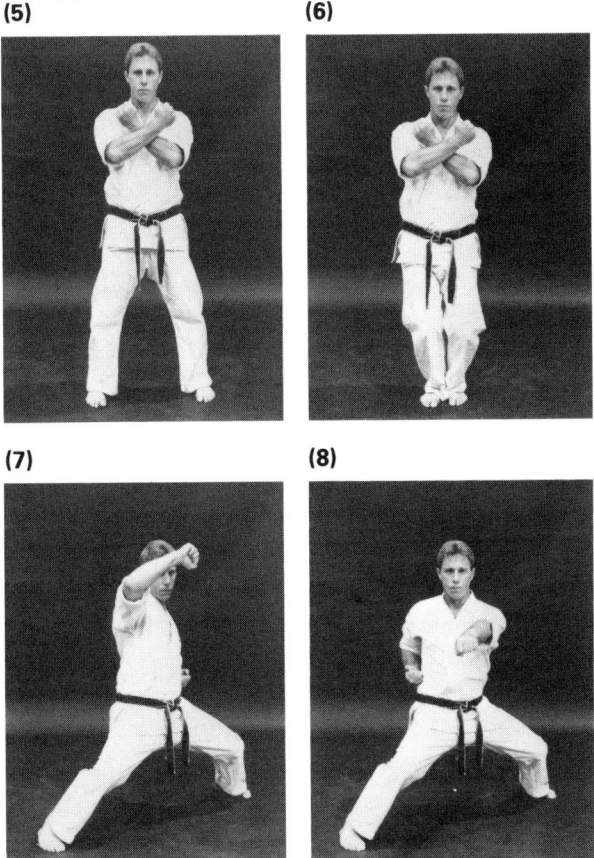

Form an X with your forearms in front of your chest, right in front of left, with the palms of both fists facing your body. **(5)**

Step back with your left foot to your left rear at a 45-degree angle into an immovable stance. **(6)** Execute a right rising high block with your torso in a half-front-facing position and your left fist on your left hip. **(7)**

Rotate your shoulders as you execute a middle level reverse punch with your left hand. **(8)** Return to the starting position.

Ten-No-Kata Technique Number 10

Technique: High Outside Block (jōdan soto uki)
　　　　　　Middle Level Reverse Punch (chūdan gyaku-zuki)

Stance: Immovable Stance (fudō-dachi)

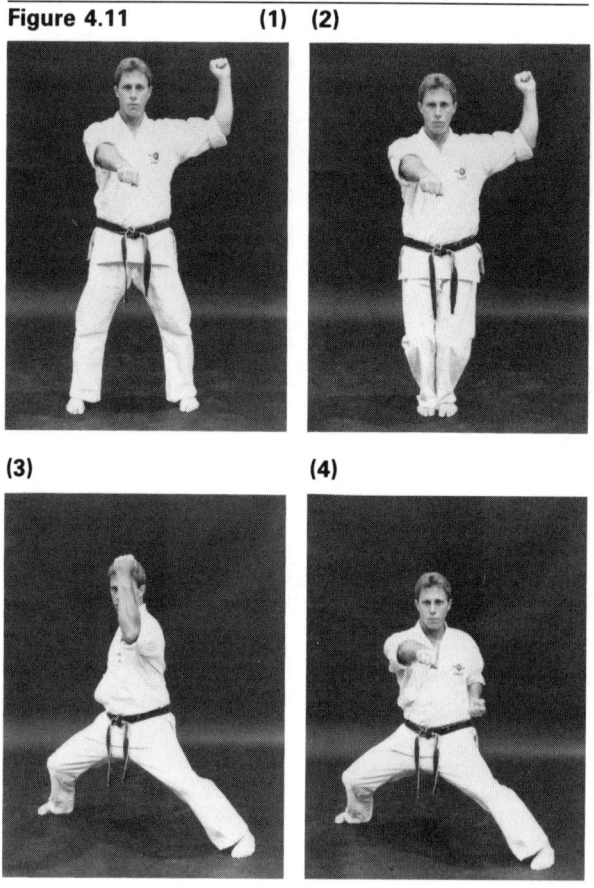

Figure 4.11

With your right arm straight, place your right fist in front of your body at mid-chest level. With your left elbow at a 90-degree angle, place your left arm to the side of your body at shoulder level so that your upper arm is horizontal and your forearm is perpendicular. **(1)**

　　Step back with your right foot to your right rear at a 45-degree angle into an immovable stance. **(2)** Immediately execute a left outside forearm high block in a half-front-facing position as you pull your right fist to your right hip. **(3)**

　　Rotate your shoulders as you execute a middle level reverse punch with your right hand. **(4)** Return to the starting position.

With your left arm straight, place your left fist in front of your body at mid-chest level. With your right elbow at a 90-degree angle, place your right arm to the side of your body at shoulder level so that your upper arm is horizontal and your forearm is perpendicular. **(5)**

Step back with your left foot to your left rear at a 45-degree angle into an immovable stance. **(6)** Immediately execute a right outside forearm high block in a half-front-facing position as you pull your left fist to your left hip. **(7)**

Rotate your shoulders as you execute a middle level reverse punch with your left hand. **(8)** Return to the starting position.

Kata (Formal Exercises)

For the remaining katas study the sequence photographs, then walk through each kata step by step using the description, the performance line, and the sequence photographs. As you come to understand the general pattern of the kata it may be helpful to have someone read the description to you as you go through the kata.

Each kata is progressively more complex and more difficult to perform. They should be learned in the following order:

1. Ten-No-Kata
2. Taikyoku Shōdan
3. Taikyoku Nidan
4. Taikyoku Sandan
5. Heian Shōdan
6. Heian Nidan
7. Heian Sandan
8. Heian Yondan
9. Heian Godan

Taikyoku Shōdan

Position	Stance	Technique
Yōi		
1	Left Front Stance	Left Down Block
2	Right Front Stance	Middle Level Right Lunge Punch
3	Right Front Stance	Right Down Block
4	Left Front Stance	Middle Level Left Lunge Punch
5	Left Front Stance	Left Down Block
6	Right Front Stance	Middle Level Right Lunge Punch
7	Left Front Stance	Middle Level Left Lunge Punch
8	Right Front Stance	Middle Level Right Lunge Punch (Kiai)
9	Left Front Stance	Left Down Block
10	Right Front Stance	Middle Level Right Lunge Punch
11	Right Front Stance	Right Down Block
12	Left Front Stance	Middle Level Left Lunge Punch
13	Left Front Stance	Left Down Block
14	Right Front Stance	Middle Level Right Lunge Punch
15	Left Front Stance	Middle Level Lunge Punch
16	Right Front Stance	Middle Level Right Lunge Punch (Kiai)
17	Left Front Stance	Left Down Block
18	Right Front Stance	Middle Level Right Lunge Punch
19	Right Front Stance	Right Down Block
20	Left Front Stance	Middle Level Left Lunge Punch (Kiai)

Figure 4.12 Taikyoku Shōdan Embusen

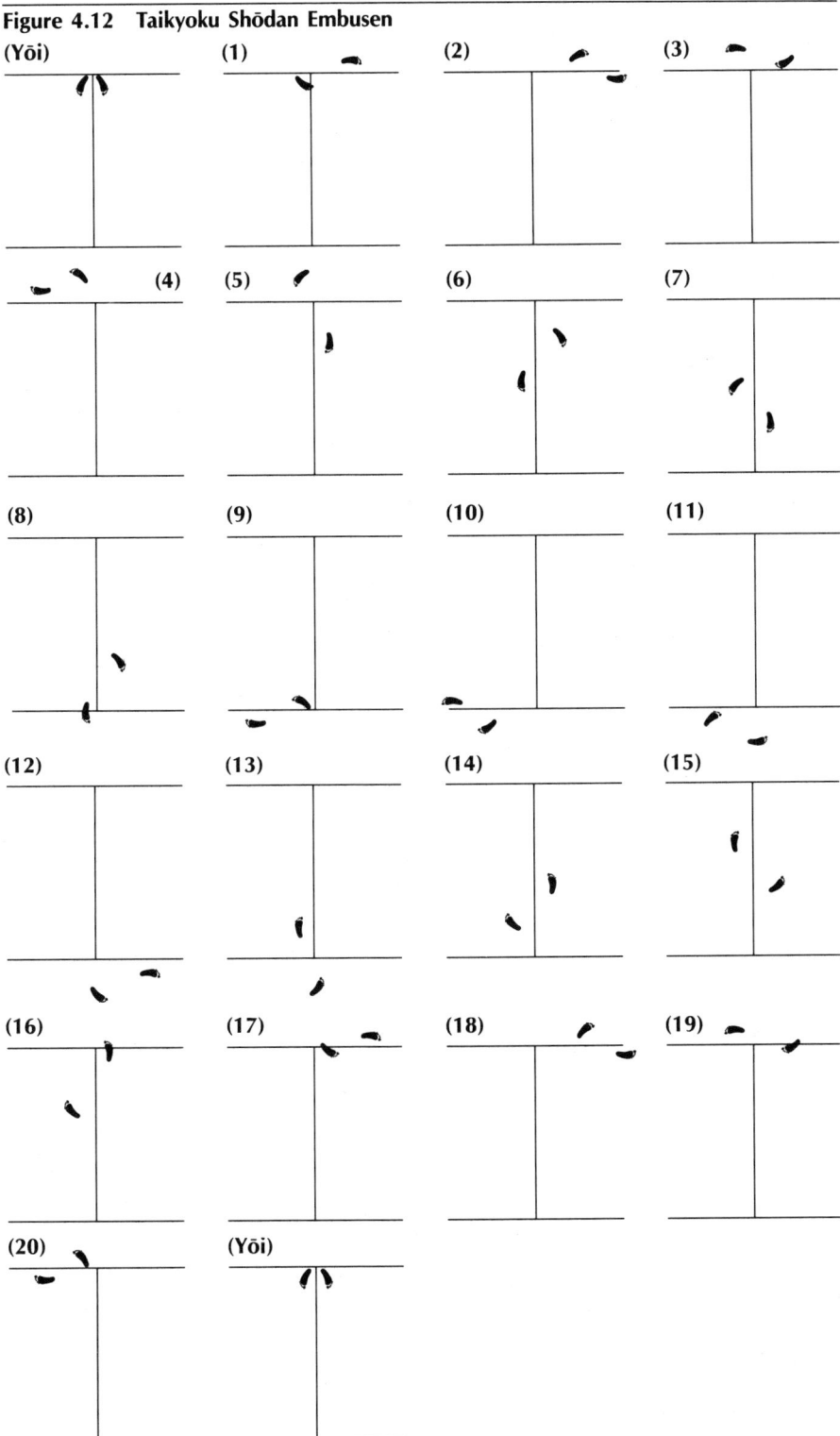

Kata (Formal Exercises)

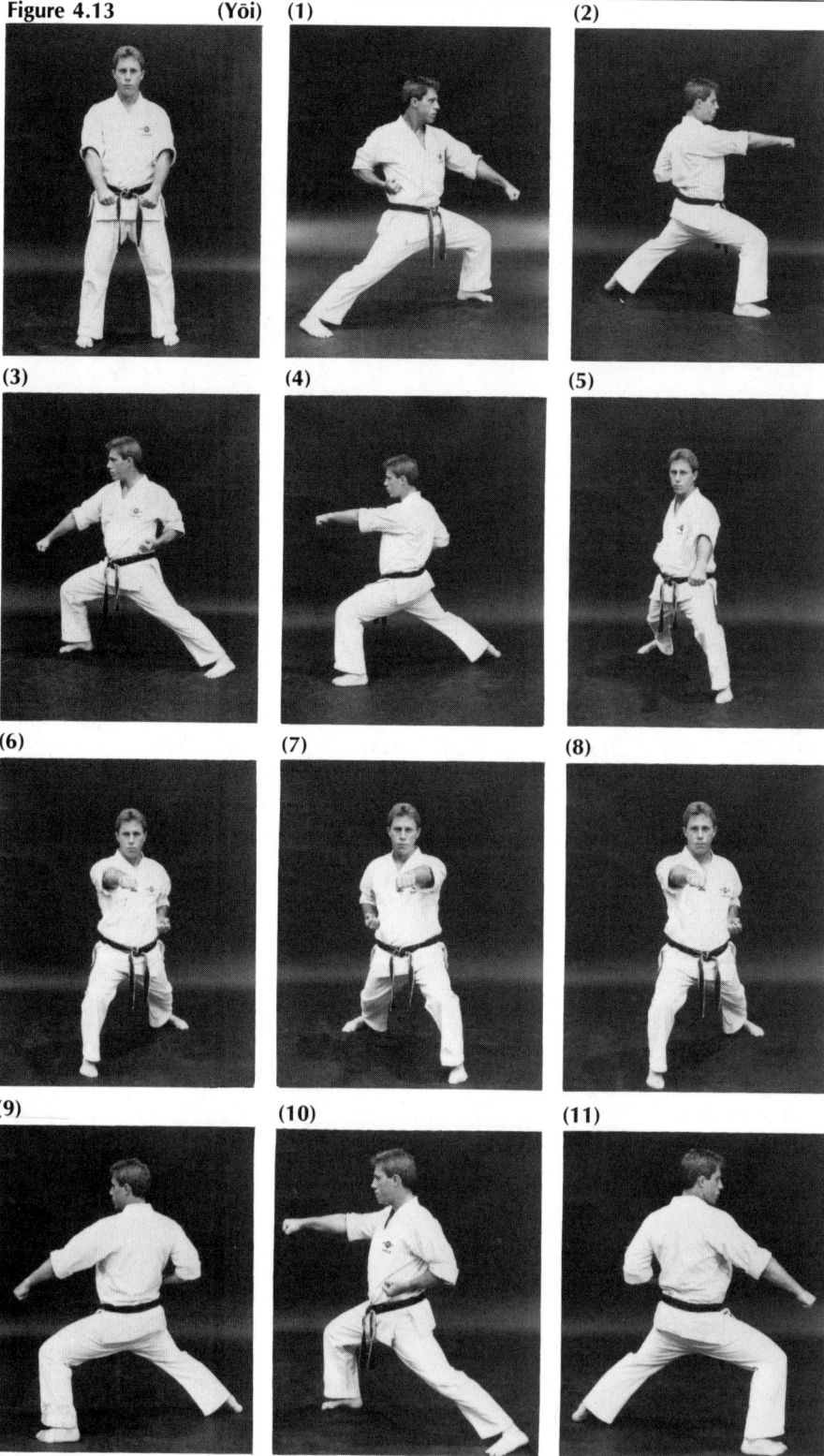

Figure 4.13

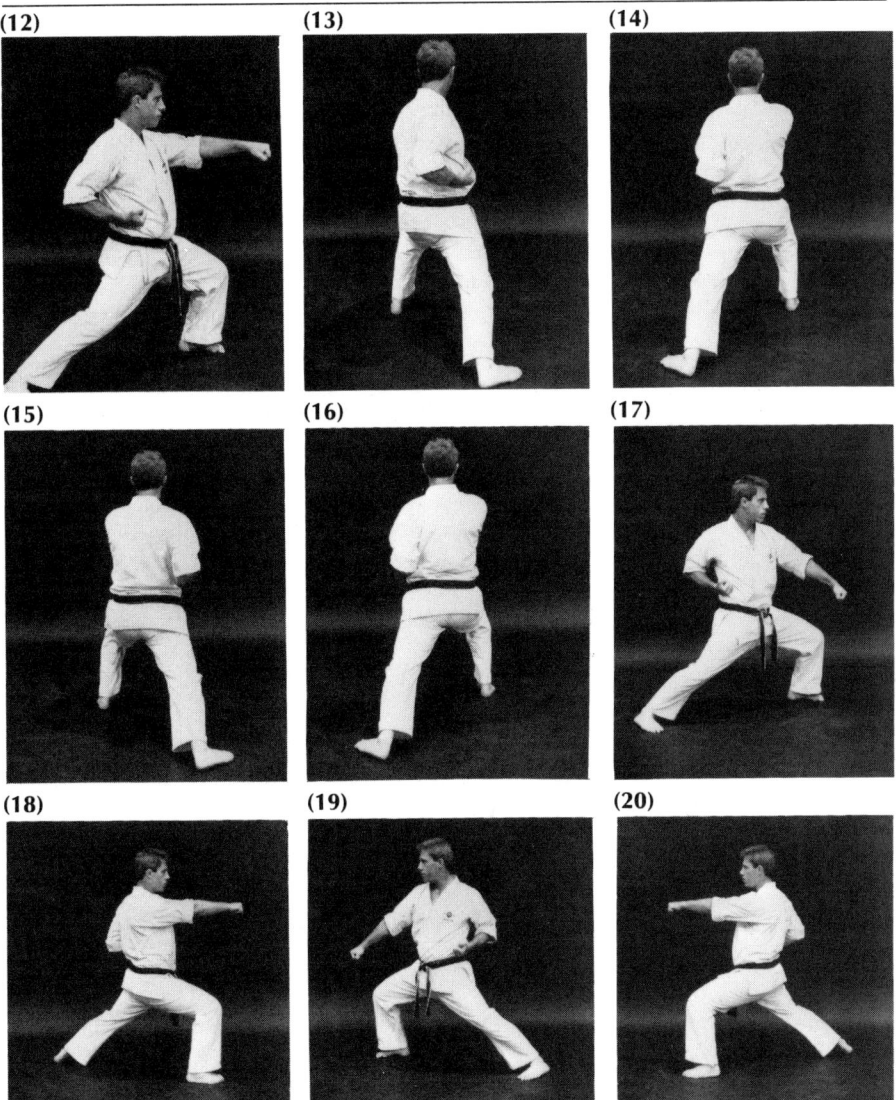

Taikyoku Nidan

Taikyoku Nidan is the same as Taikyoku Shōdan except that all the punches are upper level instead of middle level.

Taikyoku Sandan

Taikyoku Sandan is the same as Taikyoku Shōdan except that the front stances with down blocks (techniques 1, 3, 9, 11, 17, and 19) are replaced with back stances and middle level chest blocks. Also, the middle level lunge punches (techniques 6, 7, 8, 14, 15, and 16) are replaced with upper level lunge punches.

Kata (Formal Exercises)

Heian Shōdan

Position	Stance	Technique
Yōi		
1	Left Front Stance	Left Down Block
2	Right Front Stance	Right Middle Level Punch
3	Right Front Stance	Right Down Block
4	T-Stance	Hammer Fist Strike
5	Left Front Stance	Left Middle Level Punch
6a	Left Front Stance	Combination Left Down Block With Left
6b		Open Hand High Block
7	Right Front Stance	High Block
8	Left Front Stance	High Block
9	Right Front Stance	High Block (Kiai)
10	Left Front Stance	Left Down Block

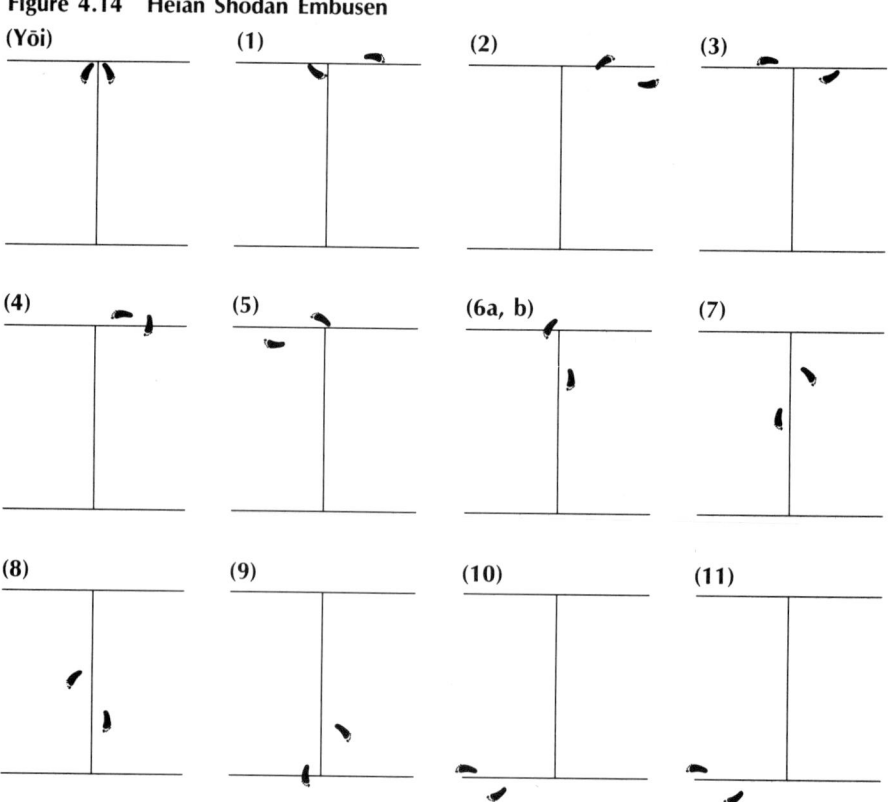

Figure 4.14 Heian Shōdan Embusen

Position	Stance	Technique
11	Right Front Stance	Right Middle Level Punch
12	Right Front Stance	Right Down Block
13	Left Front Stance	Left Middle Level Punch
14	Left Front Stance	Left Down Block
15	Right Front Stance	Right Middle Level Punch
16	Left Front Stance	Left Middle Level Punch
17	Right Front Stance	Right Middle Level Punch (Kiai)
18	Right Back Stance	Left Middle Level Knife Hand Block
19	Left Back Stance	Right Middle Level Knife Hand Block
20	Left Back Stance	Right Middle Level Knife Hand Block
21	Right Back Stance	Left Middle Level Knife Hand Block

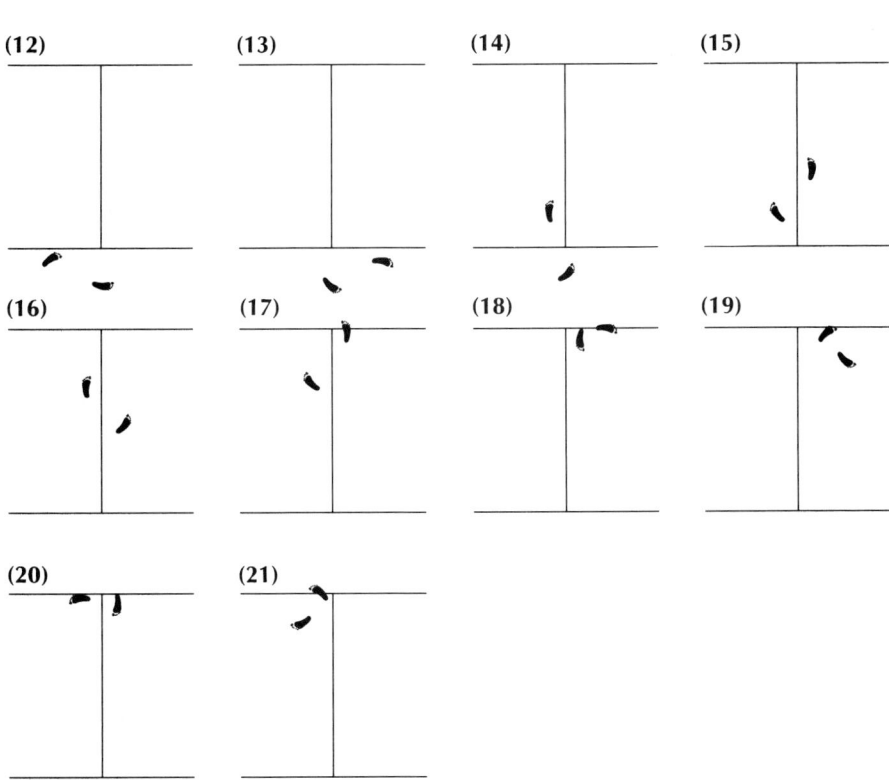

Kata (Formal Exercises)

Figure 4.15

Heian Nidan

Position	Stance	Technique
Yōi		
1a	Right Back Stance	Left Arm High Block and Right Arm Side Guard
1b		Left Arm Sweep Block and Right Hand Hammer Fist
1c		Left Straight Punch and Right Fist to Hip
2a	Left Back Stance	Right Arm High Block and Left Arm Side Guard
2b		Right Arm Sweep Block and Left Hand Hammer Fist
2c		Right Straight Punch and Left Fist to Hip
3	Left Leg Stance	Right Middle Level Side Kick and Right Back Fist to Face (Kiai)
4	Right Back Stance	Middle Level Right Knife Hand Block
5	Left Back Stance	Middle Level Left Knife Hand Block
6	Right Back Stance	Middle Level Right Knife Hand Block
7a	Left Front Stance	Left Hand Pressing Block

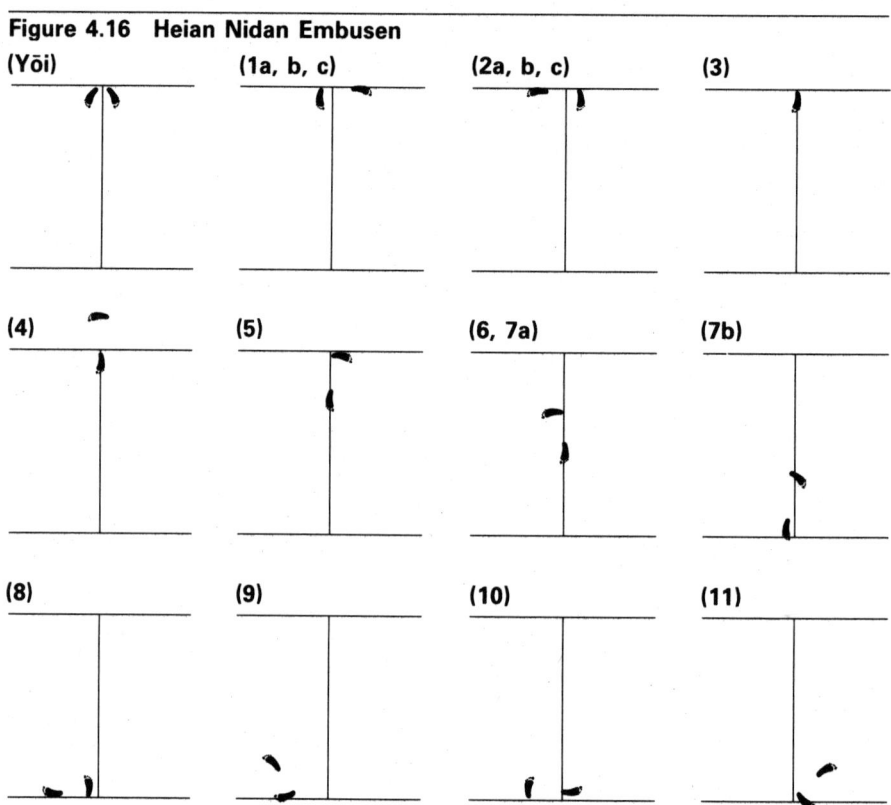

Figure 4.16 Heian Nidan Embusen

Position	Stance	Technique
7b	Right Front Stance	Middle Level Right Spearhand
8	Right Back Stance	Middle Level Knife Hand Block
9	Left Back Stance	Middle Level Right Knife Hand Block
10	Left Back Stance	Middle Level Right Knife Hand Block
11	Right Back Stance	Middle Level Left Knife Hand Block
12a	Left Front Stance	Middle Level Right Inside Block
12b		Middle Level Right Front Kick
13	Right Front Stance	Middle Level Left Hand Reverse Punch
14a		Middle Level Right Inside Block
14b		Middle Level Left Front Kick
15	Left Front Stance	Middle Level Right Hand Reverse Punch
16	Right Front Stance	Middle Level Augmented Forearm Block (Kiai)
17	Left Front Stance	Left Down Block
18	Right Front Stance	Right Forearm High Block
19	Right Front Stance	Right Down Block
20	Left Front Stance	Left Forearm High Block (Kiai)

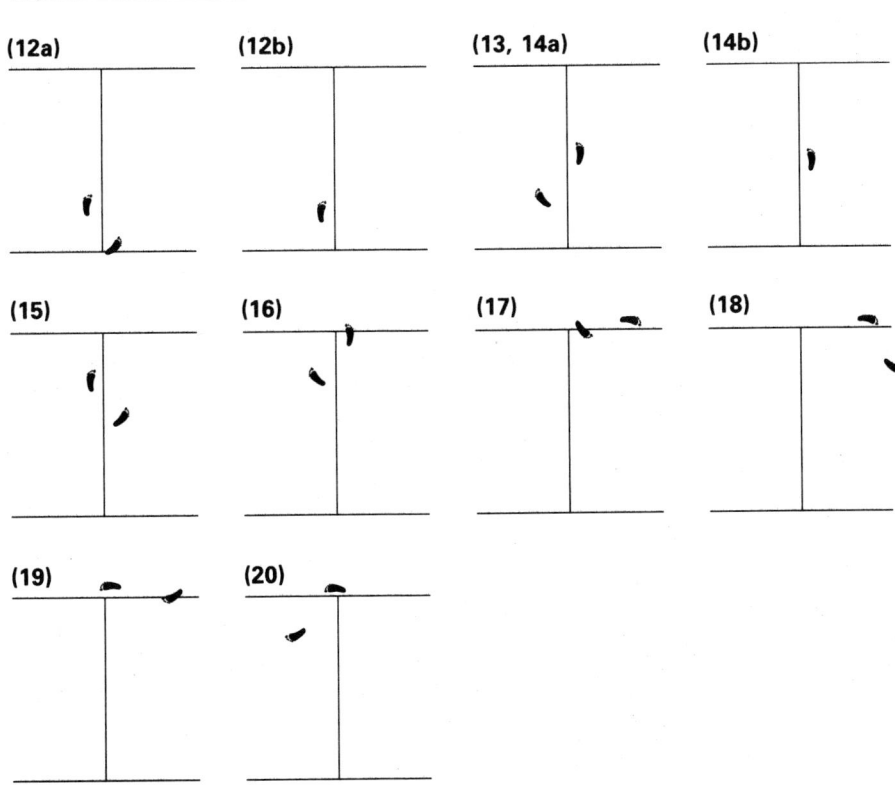

Kata (Formal Exercises)

Figure 4.17

82　　　　　　　　　　　　　　　　　　　　　　　　　　　　　　　　KARATE

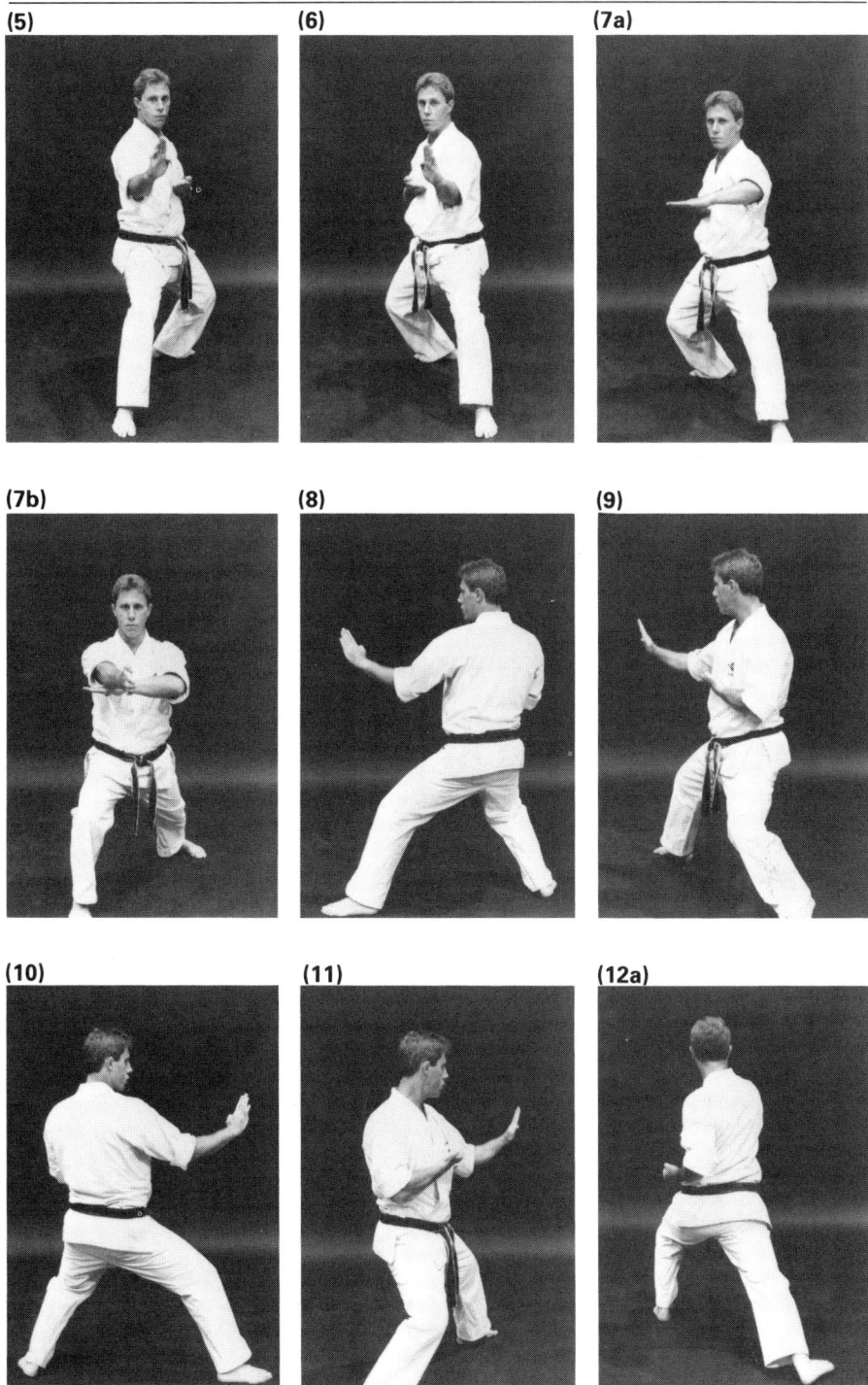

Kata (Formal Exercises)

Figure 4.17 (cont'd)

(12b)  (13)

(14a)  (14b)

(15)

Kata (Formal Exercises)

Heian Sandan

Position	Stance	Technique
Yōi		
1	Right Back Stance	Middle Level Left Chest Block
2a	Closed-Feet Stance	Right Middle Inside Block and Left Down
2b		Block then Left Middle Inside Block and Right Down Block
3	Left Back Stance	Middle Level Right Chest Block
4a	Closed-Feet Stance	Left Middle Inside Block and Right Down
4b		Block then Right Middle Inside Block and Left Down Block
5	Right Back Stance	Double Forearm Middle Level Block
6	Right Front Stance	Left Hand Pressing Block with Right Hand Middle Spear Hand
7	Straddle Stance	Left Hammer Fist Strike to Body
8	Right Front Stance	Right Middle Level Lunge Punch (Kiai)
9a	Closed-Feet Stance	Side Guard Position with Both Fists
9b	Transition Step	(front view)

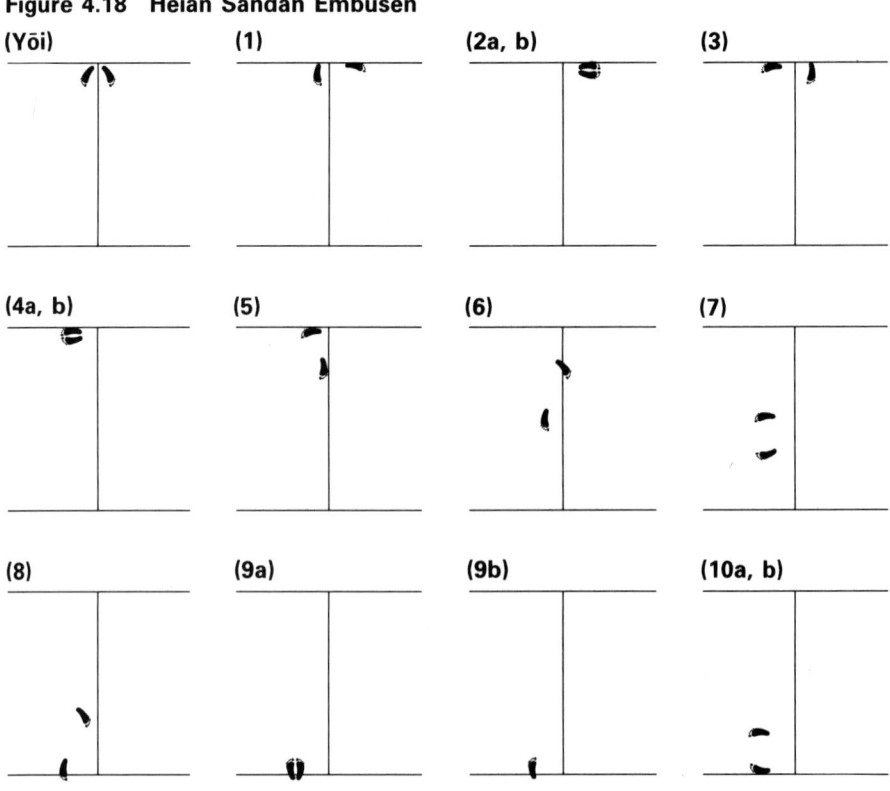

Figure 4.18 Heian Sandan Embusen

86   KARATE

Position	Stance	Technique
10a	Straddle Stance	Right Foot Stomp Kick with Right Elbow
10b		Block and Right Hand Upper Level Back Fist
11a	Straddle Stance	Left Foot Stomp Kick with Left Elbow Block and
11b		Left Hand Upper Level Back Fist
12a	Straddle Stance	Right Foot Stomp Kick with Right Elbow Block and
12b		Right Hand Upper Level Back Fist followed
12c		by Middle Level Right Vertical
12d	(side view)	Knife Hand Block
13	Left Front Stance	Left Middle Level Lunge Punch (Kiai)
14	Straddle Stance	Right Hand Upper Level Thrust with Left Elbow Strike to Rear
15	Straddle Stance	Left Hand Upper Level Thrust with Right Elbow Strike to Rear (Kiai)

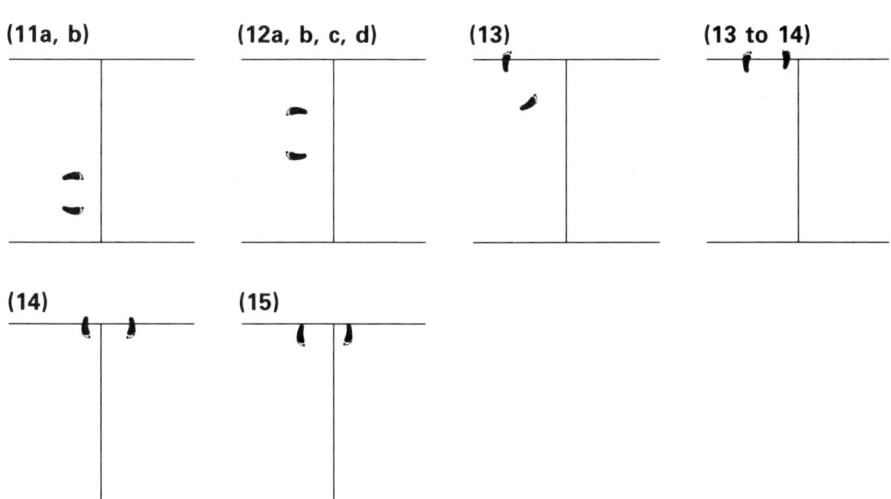

Kata (Formal Exercises)

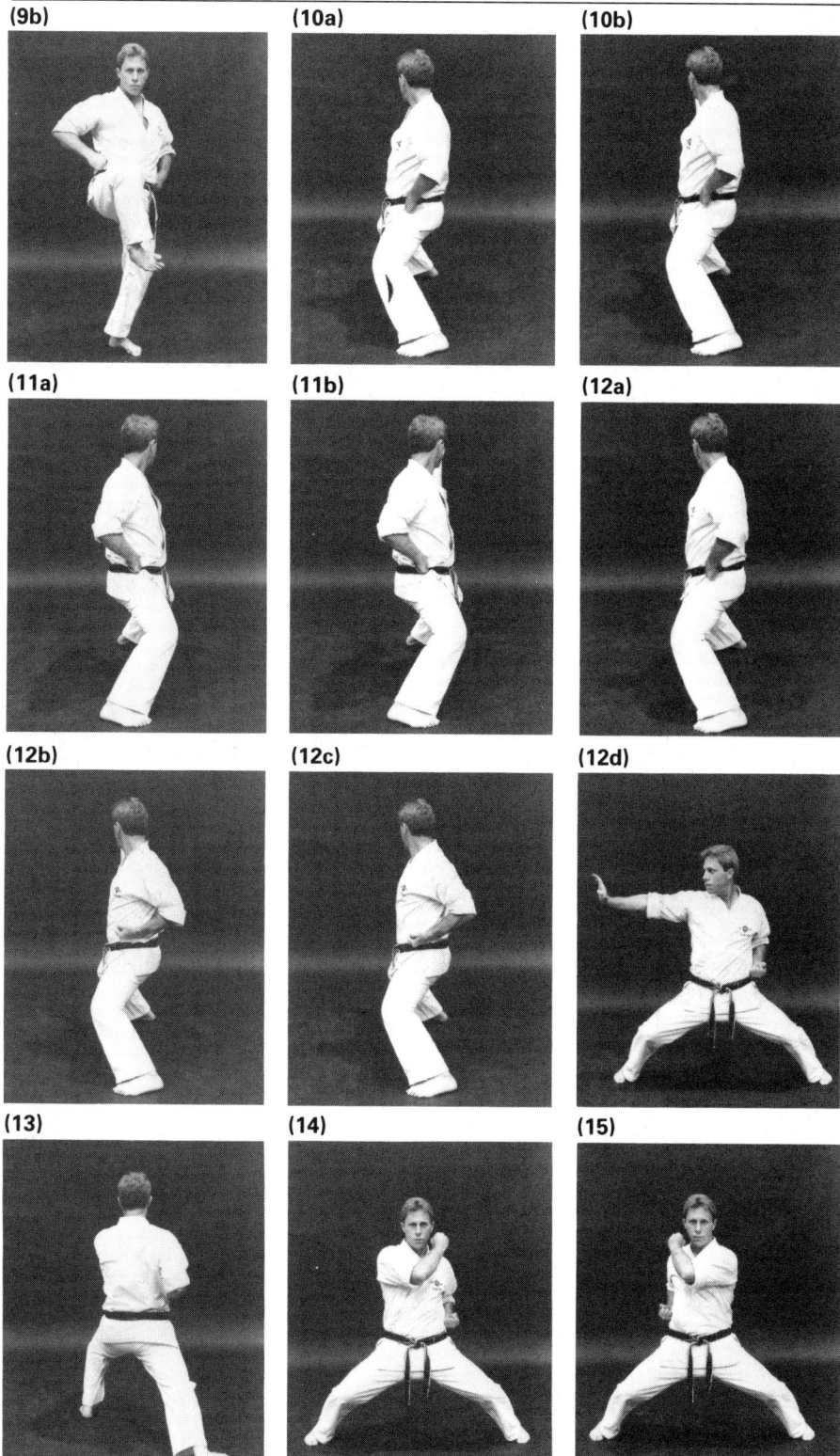

Heian Yondan

Position	Stance	Technique
Yōi		
1	Right Back Stance	Left Open Hand Forearm Face Block with Right Hand Upper Level Guard Position
2	Left Back Stance	Right Open Hand Forearm Face Block with Left Hand Upper Level Guard Position
3	Left Front Stance	Lower Level X-Block
4	Left Back Stance	Double Forearm Middle Level Block
5a	Right Leg Stance	Two Fist Right Side Guard Position
5b		Left Leg Middle Level Side Kick with Left Back Fist to Face
6	Left Front Stance	Right Elbow Strike
7a	Left Leg Stance	Two Fist Left Side Guard Position
7b		Right Leg Middle Level Kick with Right Back Fist to Face
8	Right Front Stance	Left Elbow Strike
9a	Parallel Foot Stance	Left Open Hand Upper Block with Right
9b		Knife Hand Strike to Neck followed

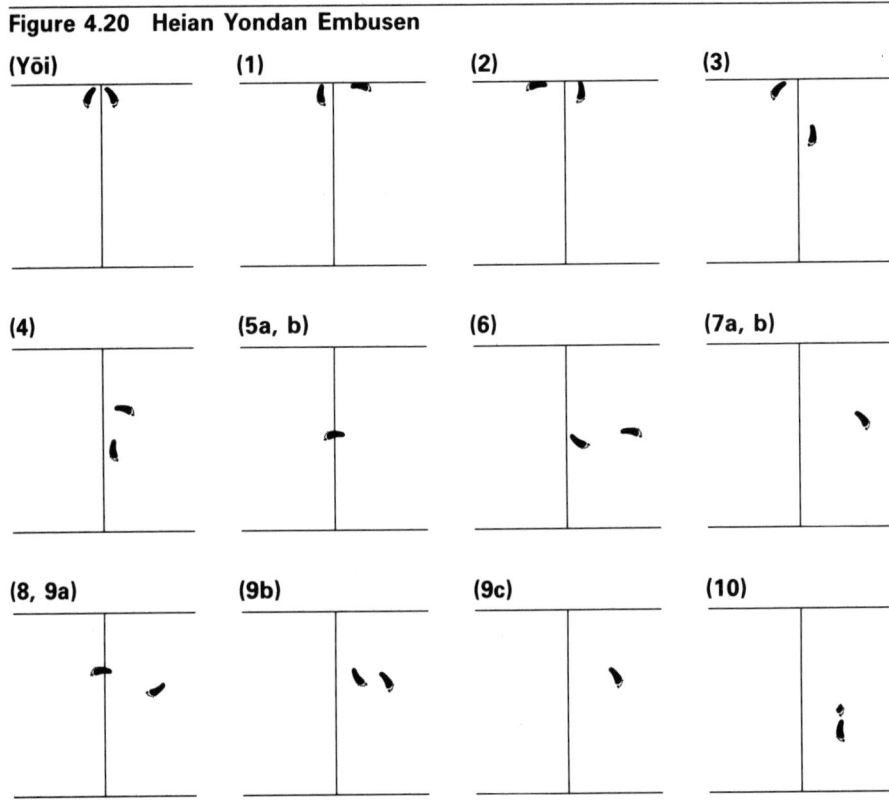

Figure 4.20 Heian Yondan Embusen

Position	Stance	Technique
9c		with Right Front Kick to Face
10	Right Foot Stance	Right Back Fist
11a, b	Left Front Stance	Middle Level Reverse Wedge Block with
11c		Middle Level Right Leg Front Kick
12a	Right Front Stance	Right Middle Level Lunge Punch and
12b		Left Middle Level Reverse Punch
13a, b	Right Front Stance	Middle Level Reverse Wedge Block with
13c		Middle Level Left Leg Front Kick
14a	Left Front Stance	Left Middle Level Lunge Punch and
14b		Right Middle Level Reverse Punch
15	Right Back Stance	Double Forearm Middle Level Block
16	Left Back Stance	Double Forearm Middle Level Block
17a	Right Back Stance	Double Forearm Middle Level Block with
17b		Right Knee Strike
18	Right Back Stance	Middle Level Left Knife Hand Block
19	Left Back Stance	Middle Level Right Knife Hand Block (Kiai)

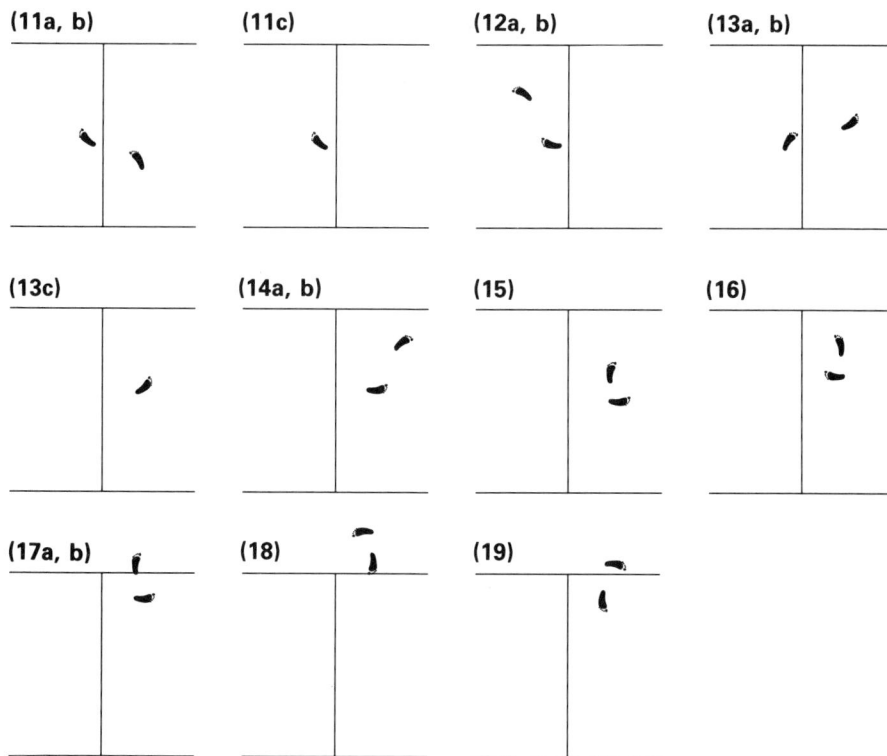

Kata (Formal Exercises)

Kata (Formal Exercises)

93

Figure 4.21 (cont'd)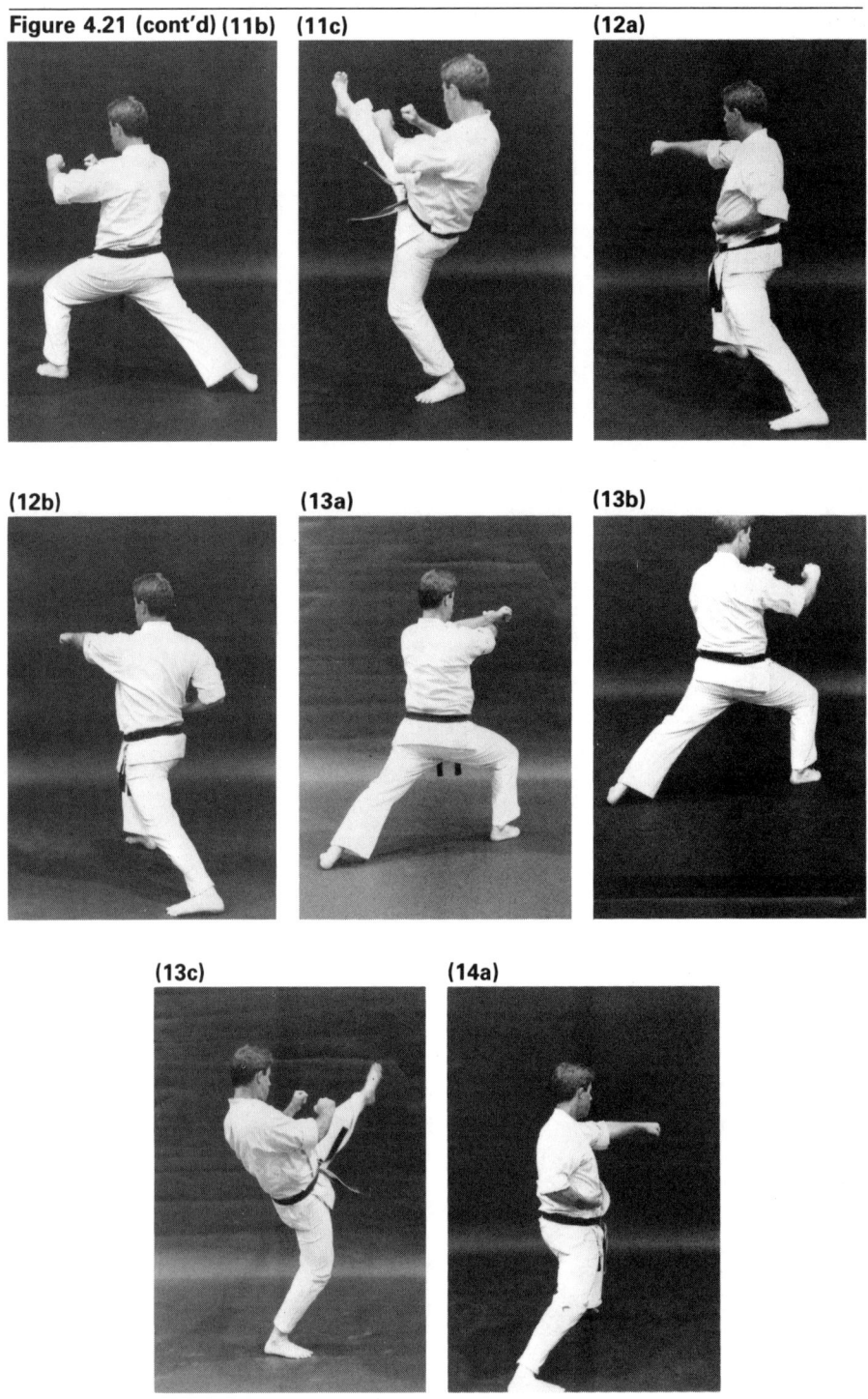

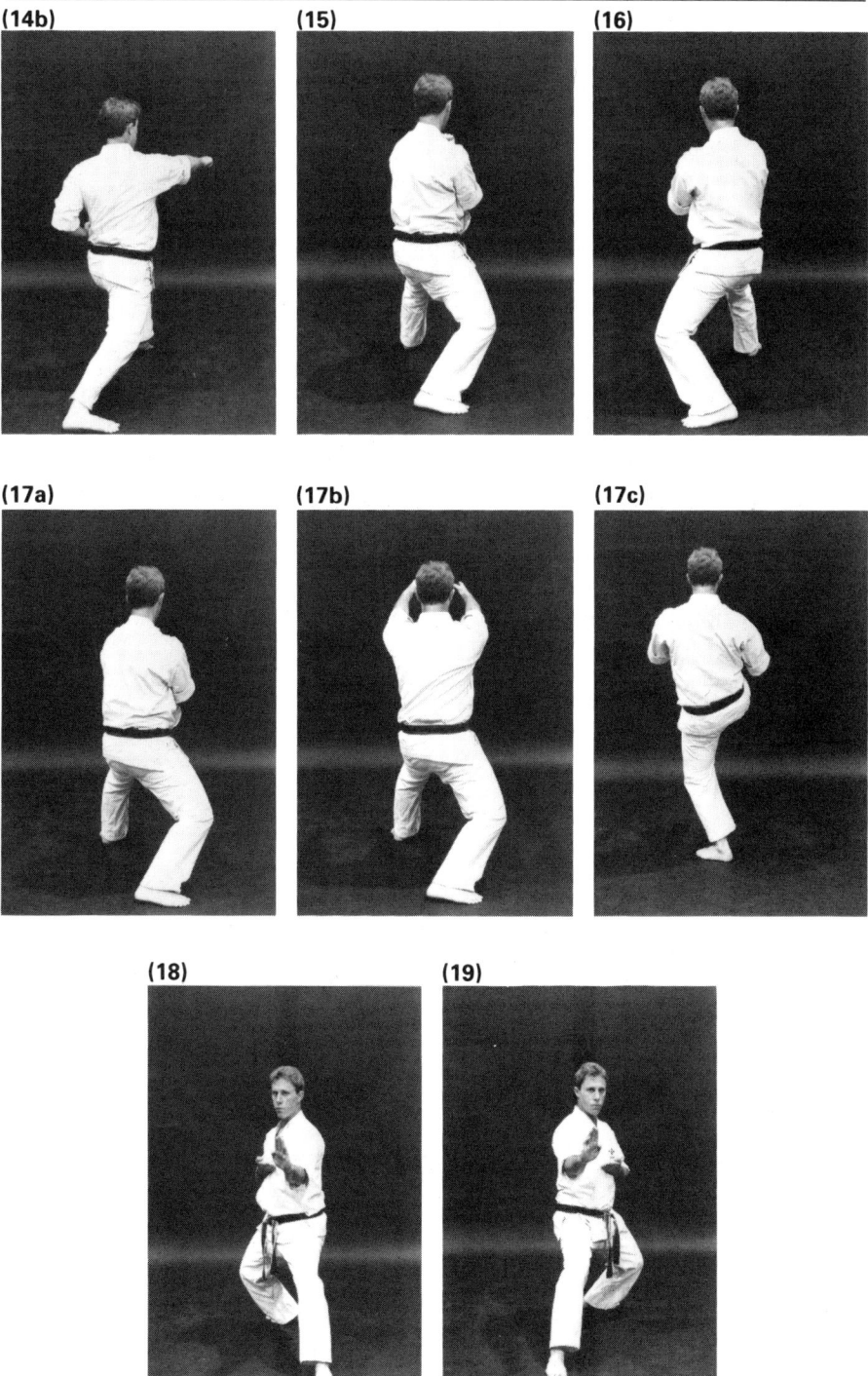

Kata (Formal Exercises)

Heian Godan

Position	Stance	Technique
Yōi		
1a	Right Back Stance	Middle Level Left Chest Block with
1b		Right Middle Level Reverse Punch
2	Closed-Feet Stance	Left Forearm with Right Fist Guard Position
3a	Left Back Stance	Middle Level Right Chest Block with
3b		Left Middle Level Reverse Punch
4	Closed-Feet Stance	Right Forearm with Left Fist Guard Position
5	Left Back Stance	Double Forearm Middle Level Block
6a	Left Front Stance	Lower Level X-Block with
6b		Open Two Hand Upper Level X-Block with
6c		Fist Punch to Body
7	Right Front Stance	Middle Level Right Lunge Punch (Kiai)
8a	Straddle Stance	Right Down Block with Stomping Kick
8b		Left Hand Hooking Block with
8c		Right Foot Crescent Kick
9	Straddle Stance	Right Elbow Strike
10	Right Foot Stance	Double Forearm Middle Level Block

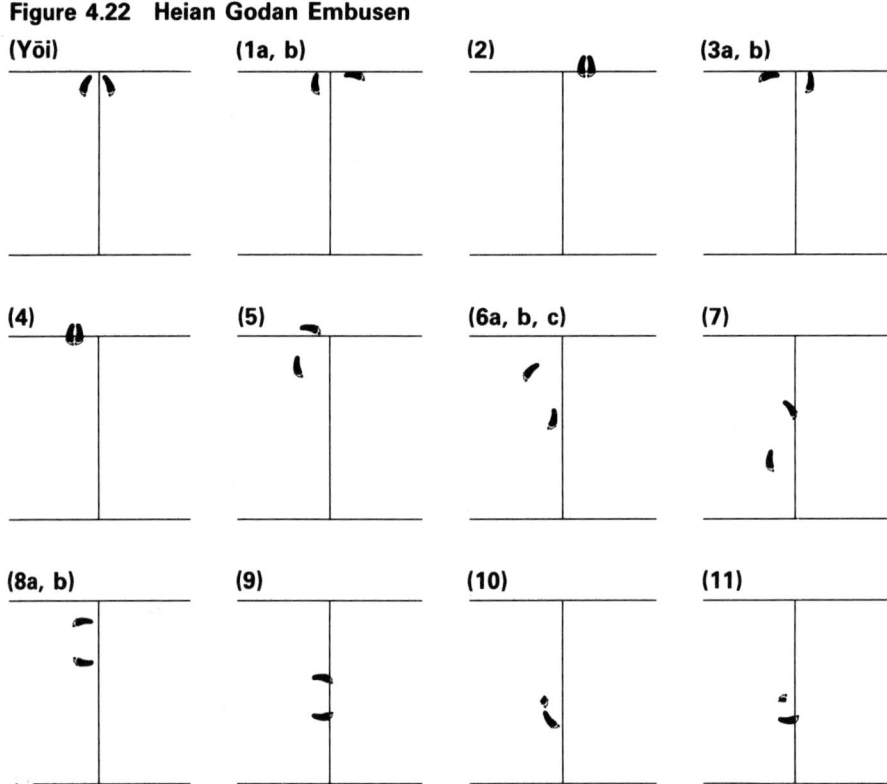

Figure 4.22 Heian Godan Embusen

Position	Stance	Technique
11	L-Stance	Right Double Fist Upward Strike with Jumping Left 90-degree Turn (Kiai)
12	Right Foot Stance	Lower Level X-Block
13	Right Front Stance	Double Forearm Middle Level Block with
14a		Turning Lower Right Knife Hand Blow and Left Hand Right Shoulder Block to Left Front Stance
14b	Right Back Stance	Right Upper Level Striking Block with Left Lower Level Down Block
15	Closed-Feet Stance	Same Hand Position as 14, then 180-degree Left Turn with Left Upper Level Striking Block and Vertical Right Knife Hand Block followed by
16a		Right Front Stance with Lower Level Knife Hand Strike and Right Left Shoulder Sweeping Block
16b	Left Back Stance	Left Upper Level Striking Block with Left Lower Level Down Block (Kiai)

Kata (Formal Exercises)

Figure 4.23

Kumite (Sparring)

Kumite (sparring) is the application of the skills learned in kihon (basic techniques) and practiced in kata (formal exercises). It includes prearranged sparring and free-sparring.

Kumite provides an opportunity to practice fighting skills against an opponent without the danger of being in a life-threatening situation. During sparring practice all movements must be strictly controlled. In some forms of kumite no contact of punches, strikes, or kicks is allowed. Some forms of kumite allow light contact and some kumite competitions allow full contact. Before participating in any kumite find out what rules of contact will be used.

Valuable lessons to be learned from participation in kumite include: proper distancing and timing, when to initiate an attack, early recognition of different attacks, how to defend against various attacks, and how to counterattack.

The basic forms of kumite are preplanned and carefully controlled. These forms are reasonably safe even for beginners. The more advanced forms such as jiyū-kumite (freestyle sparring) require control and judgment that come only with more karate experience.

Kumite is still in its infancy. Basic kumite was first practiced in the late 1920s after karate was introduced in Japan. During all of the centuries before that only kihon (basic techniques) and kata (formal exercises) were practiced. This new form of training is still growing and changing.

KUMITE PRINCIPLES

Keep your mind calm and your body free of tension so that you may act and react quickly and accurately.

Maintain a total awareness of your opponent rather than focusing on a small point so that you may take advantage of any opening and quickly respond to any movement.

Sanbon Kumite (Three-Step Sparring)

In sanbon kumite one opponent attacks three times in succession to the same target level using the same prearranged technique. The defender retreats and blocks each attack. After blocking the third attack the defender delivers a strong, focused counterattack. There are three target levels: upper, middle, and lower. Figure 5.1 shows the technique of sanbon kumite.

Figure 5.1 Sanbon kumite

Gohon Kumite (Five-Step Sparring)

In gohon kumite one opponent attacks five consecutive times using the same attack each time directed at the same target level. The defender moves backward blocking each attack. After blocking the last attack the defender delivers a strong, focused counterattack.

Figure 5.2 Ippon kumite

Ippon Kumite (One-Step Sparring)

Two opponents face each other in the ready stance. One opponent is the attacker while the other is the defender. The first attack is made toward the head from a front stance. As the attacker steps forward to deliver the attack the defender may step backward or forward or to the side and use an appropriate block and counter-attack. The second attack is a mid-level lunge punch and the third attack is a mid-level front kick. After these three attacks the opponents change roles. Figure 5.2 shows each step in this technique.

Kumite (Sparring)

THE SPORT EXPERIENCE

With a karate training partner try sanbon kumite, gohon kumite, and ippon kumite. Be sure that each technique to be used is understood by both of you before each attack for safety and effectiveness during training.

Do not attempt any freestyle sparring until your basic techniques are well developed and you have your instructor's approval. Freestyle can be very dangerous for beginners who do not have good basic techniques.

Jiyū-Ippon Kumite (Semi free, One-step Sparring)

Jiyū-ippon kumite serves as a transition from prearranged sparring to freestyle sparring. In jiyū-ippon kumite both opponents move around freely. One opponent attacks a prearranged target. The defender blocks the attack and delivers a counterattack.

A more advanced variation of this occurs when the attacker and defender are predetermined but the method of attack and the target are not.

Jiyū Kumite (Freestyle Sparring)

In jiyū kumite both opponents move about freely. Either opponent can attack at any time using any technique. The sparring continues until someone scores a focused attack on a vital target. During jiyū kumite all punches, strikes, and kicks are stopped just short of contact. The ability to deliver these techniques with maximum power, speed, and control, without injuring your training partner, requires long hours of intense, repetitive, precise training and conditioning.

There are many forms of free-sparring. In one variation all attacks are performed slowly. In another variation attacks are performed quickly but with less than maximum power. There is also kick sparring in which only the feet are used and hand sparring in which only the hands are used. All of the variations of sparring have a purpose and each variation will add something of value to your total karate training program.

Enjin Kumite (Circle Sparring)

In enjin kumite one person is located in the center of a circle of attackers, usually six to eight attackers. The objective of each attacker is to deliver a single, powerful attacking technique to the opponent in the center of the circle. The objective of the person in the center is to move out of the line of attack, block, and counterattack. Prior to each attack an attacker on the perimeter of the circle signals with a verbal warning (chūi). The person in the center replies immediately with a verbal response and warning (chūi). The attack, block, and counterattack sequence immediately follow the reply.

In one advanced variation of enjin kumite, the attacker gives a verbal warning but does not have to wait for a reply from the defender.

Another advanced variation of enjin kumite requires a verbal warning and response, but as soon as the attack is initiated, the person in the center may attack another perimeter opponent without warning, while the initial attacker passes through the center of the circle.

Suwari-Geiko Kumite (Seated Sparring)

Suwari-geiko kumite is executed from the seiza (kneeling) position with two opponents facing each other, approximately three feet apart. The first attack is a lunge punch to the face which is performed by raising up on both knees and stepping forward with one foot. The defender moves out of the line of attack and uses an appropriate block and counterattack. The second attack is a mid-level lunge punch and the third attack is a front kick. A verbal warning is given by the attacker and the defender before each attack.

Karate Progress

Progress and development in karate cannot be measured with absolute accuracy. Karate is not like an event in track and field that may be measured in centimeters or seconds, yet progress occurs. Systems of ranking, titles, and placement in competition offer some indication of your progress and reflect your development in karate.

RANK

Karate-dō uses a "kyū-dan" promotion system to assign rank. The "kyū" or "mudansha" ranks generally begin at the tenth, eighth, or sixth kyū and progress to first kyū. The color of the belt worn by the kyū ranks varies from one style of karate to another. Colors that are frequently used to indicate rank in karate include white, green, orange, yellow, blue, purple, brown, and black. The white belt usually identifies the beginner and the brown or red belt usually identifies the last colored belt rank before black belt. As a general rule the darker the color the higher the kyū rank.

The *dan* or yūdansha ranks begin at first degree black belt and progress to tenth degree black belt. In all styles of karate the dan ranks wear a black belt.

The Federation of All-Japan Karate-dō Organizations (FAJKO) uses the ranking system shown in this chapter. Other martial disciplines and other sanctioning organizations generally have a similar system. The FAJKO ranks and belt colors were presented in Chapter 2.

To progress from one rank to the next you must demonstrate improvement in skill and character. You will be tested on kihon (basic techniques), kata (formal exercises), and kumite (sparring). Some schools also require weapons kata and "tameshiwara" (board breaking). Other considerations for promotion in rank include: regular attendance at training sessions, intensity of training, knowledge of karate history, knowledge of karate philosophy, character, attitude, length of karate training, and completion of academic readings related to the martial arts.

To be considered for promotion you must be humble and willing to follow directions, put in long hours of intense practice, and demonstrate mastery of all the requirements. Understanding what is required for each rank comes only through diligent training. Therefore, the focus and approach to all training must be long and deep, never short and shallow. True progress toward perfection of skill and character requires years of disciplined training under the guidance of a qualified sensei (teacher). The progression through the colored belt ranks usually takes at least four or five years in the traditional dōjō.

There are definite differences in technical skills from first to fifth dan (black belt ranks). From sixth to tenth dan promotions are based upon technical skill plus significant contributions to the art, leadership, teaching ability, years of service to karate, and time-in-rank.

To ensure the integrity of the ranking system, advancement requires that you attain a high level of technical proficiency and maturity in each rank. Rather than meeting minimum standards students are expected to show mastery in their present rank before being considered for the next rank.

TITLES

In addition to the designated ranks, individuals may be awarded one of the three special titles as a result of exceptional achievement and outstanding character. The three special titles are Renshi, Kyōshi, and Hanshi. For the specific age, rank, and time requirements refer to the FAJKO table in Figure 6.1 (page 108).

Chief instructors of a worldwide system are known as Kancho (building head). The term Shihan (master) is given to those of 6th dan and higher. Sensei (teacher) is the title of those black belts who head an individual dōjō (training hall) or whose primary responsibility is teaching within a dōjō. Sempai (seniors) are the more experienced and higher ranking students while kōhai (juniors) are less experienced and lower ranking students. The sempai play an important role since they model appropriate behavior for the kōhai to follow.

COMPETITION

Sport competition in karate consists of two basic aspects, kata (formal exercise) and kumite (sparring).

In kata competition the karateka (karate participant) performs either a mandatory or an elective kata and is graded by one or more judges on a scale of 0 to 10. After all kata competitors have finished, the one with the highest score is the winner.

The performance of a kata is judged on form, power, speed, and the correct sequence of techniques. Integration of the body and spirit is critical as the karateka strives to demonstrate mastery of the active and passive aspects of the kata.

Kumite (sparring) competition consists of matches between two opponents of equal rank and approximately equal body weight.

Figure 6.1 Ranking system in modern Budo[1]

Ranks	Age	Title
Ju-Dan (10th) over 10 years after Ku-Dan	70 years or over	*****Hanshi** over 15 years after Kyoshi 55 years old or over
Ku-Dan (9th) 10 years after Hachi-Dan	60 years or over	
Hachi-Dan (8th) 8 years after Shichi-Dan	50 years or over	*****Kyoshi** over 10 years after Renshi 40 years old or over
Shichi-Dan (7th) 7 years after Roku-Dan	42 years or over	
Roku-Dan (6th) over 5 years after Go-Dan	35 years or over	*****Renshi** over 2 years after 5th Dan 35 years old or over
Go-Dan (5th) over 3 years after Yo-Dan	under 35 years	
Yō-Dan (4th) over 3 years after San-Dan	under 35 years	
San-Dan (3rd) over two years after Ni-Dan	under 35 years	No formal title
Ni-Dan (2nd) over 1 year after Sho-Dan	under 35 years	No formal title
Shō-Dan (1st) at least three years**	under 35 years	No formal title
Ikkyū (1st Brown) **Nikyū** (2nd Brown) **Sankyū** (3rd Brown) **Yonkyū** (4th class) **Gokyū** (5th class) **Rokkyū** (6th class) **Shichikyū** (7th class) optional **Hachikyū** (8th class) optional	No age specified	**Kyū** (below brown identified by different colors) However, all kyūs are considered white relative to the black belt

[1]Ranking system adopted by FAJKO March 27, 1971. FAJKO—Federation of All Japan Karate-Dō Organizations.
 *TITLES: May not be given irrespective of how high the rank; awarded for exceptional achievement and outstanding character.
 **Daily practice.

In noncontact karate all punches, kicks, blocks, thrusts, and strikes are used freely. Light body contact is allowed but absolutely no face contact. When a competitor reaches a valid target area using correct technique, an "ippon" (one point) is awarded. To score a point, the technique must be executed with proper balance, speed, posture, and spirit. A "waza-ari" (half-point) may be awarded when a technique is slightly lacking in any of these factors. Two out of three points wins a match. Matches usually last two to four minutes.

The center referee is responsible for the overall conduct of a match. He awards points, announces fouls, warnings, and disqualifications. One to four judges call points, when observed, and act as arbitrators if they are called upon by the referee to clarify any situation.

Mental Aspects of Karate Training

The educational system in the United States has focused primarily on mental development. In the areas of science and technology we have seen great achievement and advancement. However, this same educational system has not given equal emphasis to physical, social, emotional, spiritual, and moral development. Therefore, we find ourselves in a world in which powerful scientific knowledge may be possessed by individuals who are poorly developed emotionally, spiritually, and morally. This powerful scientific knowledge has often been misused in a destructive manner.

Every educational system is a product of the values, attitudes, and beliefs of the society in which it exists. A general attitude and belief in the United States seems to be that there is a scientific solution for every problem.

To learn karate as a scientific fighting technique that you could use to threaten or injure others, in order to establish your power over them, would be wrong. Karate should not be used to boost your ego or to establish a sense of superiority through physical intimidation of others. Karate-dō and other martial disciplines serve as methods of "seishin kyōiku" (spiritual self-cultivation).

It is important for you, as a beginning karateka, to understand some of the philosophical, psychological, and cultural aspects of the martial disciplines. This will help you to understand the true aims of karate, the training environment, the role of your teacher, the teaching process, and the attributes you will need to develop in order to make progress in karate.

THE CODE OF THE WARRIOR

The martial disciplines, because they are Oriental in nature, are reflective of some unique traditional concepts and legacies of Japanese culture. One of these legacies is the code of bushidō, whose classical concepts are somewhat emphasized in the modern martial disciplines. Bushidō (the way of the warrior) was a samurai value system that included ethical principles of loyalty, honor, justice, and benevolence. A number of individuals are attracted to karate because of their interest in learning about some of the ideas and history of the samurai warrior. This ethical code of the warrior has been an active force in the development of Japanese society.

When taught according to traditional methods, all of the martial disciplines strive to develop such ideals as loyalty, bravery, honor, acceptance of hardship, and a strong fighting spirit. Vigorous, disciplined training, which is pursued within this framework of values, attitudes, and beliefs leads toward moral and spiritual perfection. "Shūgyō" (physical and mental austerity) requires that you bear hardship calmly, make desperate efforts to persist in training, and make correct judgments in the situations that arise during training.

SPIRITUAL AND MORAL DEVELOPMENT

While societies differ concerning what they believe to be the exact characteristics that make up the ideal person, many of these characteristics are universal and cross-cultural. The Japanese martial disciplines promote the spiritual cultivation of these ideal characteristics, which are in agreement with the values of all peace-seeking societies and religions.

The highest aim of karate-dō is character development through physical, mental, and moral education. The true aim of karate-dō is to build a spiritually harmonious person with high intellect, sensitivity, and resolute will. The development of good values and enlightenment are important products of karate training.

THE MEANINGS OF KARATE-DŌ

There are many activities in Japanese culture that are devoted to the development of "seishin kyōiku" (spiritual self-cultivation). Some of the more familiar ones are Chadō (tea ceremony), Shōdō (calligraphy), and Zen meditation. The shinbudō (new martial ways) of karate-dō, kendō, jūdō, aikidō, and kyūdō are a group of disciplines that focus on self-cultivation through the combative mode. The "dō" suggests that each of these are paths or ways to travel throughout life. From a metaphysical viewpoint, these paths are understood to be moral, ethical, philosophical, and self-actualizing paths that are unending and profound and which challenge the physical and mental capacity of all participants during their lifelong pursuit of excellence and perfection.

It was Hanashiro Chomo of Okinawa, in 1905, who wrote a textbook using the new characters for karate which translate as "empty hand." The previous reading of a different ideogram with the same pronunciation was "tang" or "kara," which translated as "China" or "Chinese hand." However, it was Gichin Funakoshi, in 1933, who publicly promoted the widespread use of the translation of the word "kara" in karate-dō.

Funakoshi gave the word "kara" four meanings. The first meaning was that the art should be used as a method of empty hand self-defense. The second meaning was that the karateka should keep his mind clear or empty. Not empty of all thoughts, but clear of any evil or selfish thoughts that would interfere with the development of high ideals and values. The third meaning explains that the karateka should be like bamboo, empty or hollow on the inside yet strong, resilient, and flexible on the outside. The fourth meaning states that karate-dō is emptiness. It is compared to the emptiness of the universe. The martial disciplines all rest upon this fundamental principle. Form is emptiness and emptiness is form.

THE PRINCIPLES OF KARATE-DŌ

The following principles were given by Funakoshi as essential to true progress in karate-dō.

"Be deadly serious in training." Your opponent is always present.

"Train with your heart and soul without worrying about theory." All questions will eventually be answered through training.

"Avoid self-conceit and dogmatism." Kill ego; train, don't talk.

"Try to see yourself as you truly are and try to adopt what is meritorious in the work of others." Seek to copy good and avoid bad.

"Abide by the rules of ethics in your daily life, whether in public or in private." Always do what is morally right.

True proficiency in karate-dō lies in the application of these principles to your daily training and living. You must study and train not only with the mind and eyes of your head but also with the mind and eyes of your soul.

Method of Learning

Karate training is characterized by long, difficult hours of intense physical training. During this time the limits of your physical and mental capacities will be tested. This type of training is generally referred to as "shinshintanren" (forging of mind and body through the combative mode) and is used to develop a mature karateka.

Following the Zen format of instruction, much of the training is nonverbal and intuitive. The teacher demonstrates, rather than speaks, and you are left to discover the answers to many of your own questions following long hours of practice.

The traditional learning process with the martial disciplines is characterized by years of training under the apprenticeship of a sensei (teacher). The sensei serves two primary roles. First, the sensei provides a role model for you to follow to learn techniques, behaviors, values, attitudes, and etiquette. Second, the sensei serves as a transmitter and interpreter of the martial discipline he has practiced along with its associated culture.

The social organization in the martial disciplines is a reflection of the social organization that exists in Japanese society in general. The relationship that exists between the sensei and student is paternalistic. This relationship is based on personal loyalty and a complex system of reciprocal obligations. The bond between teacher and student is based more on personal discipleship than on group membership.

Levels of Development

The first level of training is known as "gyō." At this level you will be introduced to the fundamentals of karate: the techniques, customs, and etiquette. At this level you will be given no latitude. You must practice the techniques repeatedly over long periods of time. Your teacher may seem overly critical and demanding. You are meant to learn self-discipline, patience, and perseverance at this stage.

The second level of training is known as "shūgyō" (physical and mental austerity). The word indicates rigorous training in religious austerities. During this stage the martial disciplines take on a quasi-spiritual nature. At this stage you will have a good foundation of basic techniques and your focus will be on uninterrupted training.

The third level is known as the "jutsu" level or art stage. At this stage you will have mastery of the basic skills and will be able to perform almost all the techniques subconsciously. While proficient, you will still be able to see the need to polish your technique.

The fourth level is known as the "dō" level. At this level you will transcend the outer forms physically and spiritually. This is a stage of self-actualization or self-realization. It is this stage that is the equivalent of the Zen satori (enlightenment).

Words are inadequate to explain some of life's experiences. How can you explain the colors of a rainbow to someone who has been blind from birth? How can you explain the taste of a strawberry to someone who has never tasted one? How can you explain nuclear physics to a one-year-old child? How can you explain the highest level mental aspects of karate to someone who does not have the experience to understand?

This book began by saying, "Karate begins in your mind." If you follow this rigorous path toward spiritual self-cultivation and physical self-perfection you will find that karate also ends in your mind. That is not to say you will be back where you started, quite the contrary, you will have learned a great deal during your karate-dō journey, not only about karate techniques, but about yourself as well.

Appendix A
Glossary (Japanese/English)

Counting

Ichi	One	Roku	Six
Ni	Two	Shichi	Seven
San	Three	Hachi	Eight
Shi	Four	Kū	Nine
Go	Five	Jū	Ten

Directions

Mae	Front	Yasume	Relax
Ushiro	Back	Narande	Line up
Hidari	Left	Seiretsu	Line up by rank
Migi	Right	Modotte	Return to original position
Hajime	Begin		
Yame	Stop	Rei	Bow
Yōi	Ready	Sensei ni rei	Bow to teacher
Mawatte	Turn	Ōtagai ni rei	Bow to each other

Tachikata (Stances)

Fudō-dachi	Immovable stance	Neko-ashi-dachi	Cat stance
Hachiji-dachi	Open-leg stance	Renōji-dachi	L-stance
Hangetsu-dachi	Half-moon stance	Sanchin-dachi	Hourglass stance
Heikō-dachi	Parallel stance	Shiko-dachi	Square stance
Heisoku-dachi	Informal attention stance	Shizentai	Natural position
		Sochin-dachi	Diagonal straddle-leg stance
Jiyū-dachi	Freestyle stance		
Kiba-dachi	Straddle stance	Teiji-dachi	T-stance
Kōkutsu-dachi	Back stance	Uchi-hachiji-dachi	Inverted open-leg stance
Musubi-dachi	Informal attention stance	Zenkutsu-dachi	Forward stance

Tsukiwaza (Punching Techniques)

Age-zuki	Rising punch	Kizami-zuki	Jab
Awase-zuki	U-punch	Morote-zuki	Double fist punch
Choku-zuki	Straight punch	Nagashi-zuki	Flowing punch
Dan-zuki	Consecutive punching	Nakadaka-ippon-ken	Middle finger one knuckle fist
Gyaku-zuki	Reverse punch	Oi-zuki	Lunge punch
Hiraken-zuki	Fore-knuckle fist straight punch	Seiken-choku-zuki	Fore-fist straight punch
Hasami-zuki	Scissors punch	Tate-zuki	Vertical fist punch
Keiko-zuki	Parallel punch	Teishō-zuki	Palm-heel punch
Ippon-ken-zuki	One-knuckle fist straight punch	Ura-zuki	Close punch
		Yama-zuki	Wide U-punch
Kagi-zuki	Hook punch		

Uchiwaza (Striking Techniques)

Empi-uchi	Elbow strike	Nukite	Spear hand
Haishu-uchi	Back-hand strike	Riken-uchi	Back-fist strike
Haitō-uchi	Ridge-hand strike	Shūtō-uchi	Knife-hand strike
Hiji-uchi	Elbow strike	Tettsui-uchi	Bottom-fist strike
Kentsui-uchi	Bottom-fist strike	Uraken-uchi	Back-fist strike

Keriwaza (Kicking Techniques)

Age-uke-gyaku-ashi	Upper block (reverse foot)	Mae-tobi-geri	Jumping front kick
		Mawashi-geri	Round kick
Ashibō-kake-uke	Leg hooking block	Mikazuki-geri	Crescent kick
		Nidan-geri	Double jump kick
Ashikubi-kake-uke	Angle hooking block	Sokutei-mawashi-uke	Circular sole block
Fumikiri	Cutting kick	Sokutei-osae-uke	Pressing sole block
Fumikomi	Stamping kick	Tobi-geri	Jumping kick
Gyaku-mawashi-geri	Reverse round kick	Yoko-tobi-geri	Jumping side kick
Mae-geri	Front kick		

Ukewaza (Blocking Techniques)

Age-uke	Rising block	Kake-uke	Hooking block
Gedan-barai	Downward block	Kakiwake-uke	Reverse wedge block
Haishu-uke	Back-hand block	Kakutō-uke	Bent-wrist block
Jūji-uke	X-block	Keito-uke	Chicken-head wrist

Appendix A

Morote-sukui-uke	Two-hand scooping block	Shūtō-uke	Knife-hand block
Morote-tsukami-uke	Two-hand grasping block	Sokumen-awase-uke	Side two-hand block
		Soto-uke	Outside block
Morote-uke	Augmented forearm block	Sukui-uke	Scooping block
		Teishō-awase-uke	Combined palm-heel block
Nagashi-uke	Sweeping block		
Ōsae-uke	Pressing block	Tekubi-kake-uke	Wrist-hook block
Ōtoshi-uke	Dropping block		
Ude-uke	Forearm block	Tsukami-uke	Grasping block
Seiryūto-uke	Ox-jaw hand	Uchi-uke	Inside block

Other Terms

Aite	Opponent	Ōkyu teate	First aid
Dan	Black belt rank	Osoto-gari	Major outside reap
Dōjō	Martial arts school	Ōsu	Greeting, shows respect
Embusen	Kata performance line		
		Ōuchi-gari	Major inside reap
Enjin kumite	Circle fight	Renzuki	Alternate punching
Jiyū kumite	Free sparring	Ryū	Tradition
Kamae	Posture	Sanbon kumite	Three-step sparring
Karate	Empty hand	Seiza	Formal sitting position
Kata	Formal exercise		
Kiai	Spirit cry	Sempai	Senior
Kihon	Basic exercise	Sensei	Teacher
Kohai	Junior	Shōtōkan	Pine-sea style
Kumite	Sparring	Suki	Opening
Kyū	Colored belt rank	Suwari-geiko	Seated sparring
Makiwara	Punching post	Teki	Enemy
Mokusō	Meditation	Tōri	Attacker
Nagewaza	Throwing technique	Uke	Defender
Obi	Belt	Ukemi	Falling practice

Appendix B
Pronunciation Guide (Japanese/English)

In traditional karate schools most of the techniques, and some or all of the commands, are given in the Japanese language. This guide is to assist you in the pronunciation of some of the basic Japanese terms that are used in karate. It is a transliteration based on the Hepburn Romanization system. This transliteration is a representation of the sounds of the Japanese language reproduced in the Latin alphabet as opposed to the native Japanese katakana and hiragana syllabaries.

Vowels

Letter	Sounds Like	Approximate Pronunciation
a	ah	like the *a* in father
e	eh	like the *e* in set
i	ee	like the *i* in machine
o	oh	like the *o* in go
u	oo	like the *u* in glue

Long Vowels

The pronunciation of long vowels in Japanese requires some special consideration since the meaning of some verbs change according to the length of the vowel.

Letter	Sounds Like	Approximate Pronunciation
a	a	like the *a* in day
e	e	like the *e* in tree
i	eye	like the *i* in idea
o	oh	like the *o* in snow
u	you	like the *u* in uniform

Short Vowels

The vowels *u* and *i* are sometimes short. When they are short they are not pronounced if they appear between unvoiced consonants *f, h, k, p, s, t, ch*, or *sh*. Also, when a short *u* appears at the end of a sentence after an unvoiced consonant it is not pronounced.

Consonants

Most Japanese consonants are pronounced almost the same as English consonants. The following are exceptions:

- **f** pronounced about halfway between the *h* sound and the *f* sound of English
- **g** pronounced like the *g* in go or get
- **n** pronounced like the *ng* in singer or ping-pong
- **r** pronounced between the *l* and *d* sounds of English
- **ch** pronounced like the *ch* in cherry
- **ts** pronounced like the *ts* in cuts

Double Consonants

- **kk** pronounced like the *kk* in bookkeeper
- **pp** pronounced like the *p* sounds connecting two words in English such as "skip past"
- **tt** pronounced like the *t* sounds connecting two words in English such as "test time"
- **ss** pronounced like the *s* sounds connecting two words in English such as "let's sing"

Index

Ankles, warm-up exercises for, 16–17
Attack, levels of, 34

Back kick, 50
Back stance, 26, 27, 30
Balance, 22, 24
Behavior, in karate, 9–13
Belts, 5, 6–8, 106, 107
Black belts, 106, 107
Blocks, 14, 28, 36–41, 115–16
Bodhidharma, 2
Body fat, reduction of, 19
Body parts
 as targets, 21–22
 as weapons, 19–21
Body shifting, 34
Body weight, 24
Bowing, 10–12
Buddhist monks, influence on karate development, 2
Bushidō (the way of the warrior), 110

Cardiovascular endurance, 18–19
Center block, 62
Center of gravity, and balance, 22, 24
Center spear hand thrust, 64
Character, development of, 2, 4, 111
China, influence on karate development, 2–3
Chomo, Hanashiro, 111
Chūdan (middle) level, of attack/defense, 34
Clothing, 5–8
Colors, in ranking system, 6, 8, 106
Competition, 107, 109
Contact, rules of in sparring, 100, 104, 109
Counting, Japanese/English, 114

Dan ranks, 106, 107, 108
Defense, levels of, 34
Directions, Japanese/English, 114
Dō (4th level of development), 113
Dōjō, 6, 8, 9–13
Down block, 36, 60

Ego, loss of in karate, 8, 10, 112
Elbows, warm-up exercises for, 16
Embusen (performance line), 53, 54
Enjin kumite (circle sparring), 104–5
Error Correctors
 back kick, 51
 bowing, 11
 down block, 36
 front and back stances, 31
 front kick, 46
 front-stance turns, 33–34
 high forearm block, 41
 high level lunge punch, 43
 high level reverse punch, 45
 high open hand catching block, 39
 knife hand block, 38
 middle level lunge punch, 42
 middle level reverse punch, 44
 outside forearm chest block, 37
 rising high block, 40
 round kick, 47
 side kick, 49
 stances, 28
 warm-up exercises, 17
Etiquette, in dōjō, 8, 9–13

Federation of All-Japan Karate-dō Organizations (FAJKO), 106, 107
Feet-sliding, 31
Flexibility, development of, 18
Freestyle sparring, 100, 104
Front-facing position, 28
Front kick, 46
Front stance, 25, 26, 28–29, 32, 56, 57, 58, 59
Fudō-dachi (rooted or immovable stance), 26, 27, 60, 62, 64, 66, 68, 70
Fumidashi (stepping style), 28–29
Fumikomi (stepping style), 29
Funakoshi, Gichin, 2, 111–12

Gedan (lower) level, of attack/defense, 34

Gi (uniform), 5–8
Gohon kumite (five-step sparring), 102
Gyō (1st level of training), 112–13

Hachinoji-dachi (ready stance), 25, 26
Half-front-facing position, 28
Hangetsu-dachi (wide hourglass stance), 26, 27
Hanshi, 107, 108
Heart rate, 18–19
Heian Godan, 96–99
Heian Nidan, 80–85
Heian Sandan, 86–89
Heian Shōdan, 76–79
Heian Yondan, 90–95
Heikō-dachi (parallel yōi stance), 25, 26
Heisoku-dachi (formal attention stance), 25, 26
High forearm block, 41
High level lunge punch, 43, 57
High level reverse punch, 45, 66
High open hand catching block, 39, 66
High outside block, 70
Hips, warm-up exercises for, 16
Hwa Rang Do, 3

Immovable stance, 26, 27, 60, 62, 64, 66, 68, 70
Ippon kumite (one-step sparring), 102–3

Japan, influence of karate development, 2–3, 4, 110–11, 112
Jin Heung, 3
Jiyū-ippon kumite (semi-free, one-step sparring), 104
Jiyū-kumite (freestyle sparring), 100, 104
Jōdan (upper) level, of attack/defense, 34
Jujitsu, 2, 3
Jutsu (3rd level of training), 113

Kamidana (dōjō altar), 8, 10, 12
Kancho (building head), 107

Kansha (thankfulness in student/teacher relationship), 12
Karate
  competition in, 107, 109
  development of, 2–3
  levels of development, 112–13
  method of learning, 112
  as moral and spiritual development, 110–13
  progress in, 106–9
  styles of, 3–4
  techniques of, 14–51
Karate-dō (empty-hand way), 4, 111–12
Karate-jutsu (empty-hand art or technique), 4
Karateka, deportment of, 5–13
Kata (formal exercises), 3, 5, 18, 53–99, 100, 107
Kempo, 3
Keriwaza (kicking techniques), 115
Kiba-dachi (horse stance), 26, 27
Kicks, 14, 46–51, 115
Kihon (basic techniques), 5, 14–51, 100
Knees, warm-up exercises for, 16
Knife hand block, 38, 64
Kōhai (juniors), 107
Kōkutsu-dachi (back stance), 26, 27, 30
Korea, influence on karate development, 3
Kumite (sparring), 5, 9, 11, 100–5, 107, 109
Kung Fu, 2
Kyoshi (special title), 107, 108

Middle level lunge punch, 42, 56, 103
Middle level reverse punch, 44, 58, 60, 62, 68, 70
Moral development, karate as, 2, 4, 110–13
Muscle contractions, 24
Muscle endurance, development of, 18
Muscles, warming of, 17–18
Musubi-dachi (informal attention stance), 25, 26

Naha-te school of karate, 3
Neck, warm-up exercises for, 15
Neko-ashi-dachi (cat stance), 26, 27

Obi (belt), 5, 6–8

Okinawa, influence on karate development, 2–3
Okinawan Te school of karate, 3
Outside forearm chest block, 37

Performance line, 53, 54
Physical conditioning, 18–19
Prearranged sparring, 100–4
Promotion in rank, 106–7, 108
Pronunciation, Japanese/English, 117–18
Punches, 14, 28, 42–45, 115

Ranks, 12, 106–7, 108
Reigi saho (etiquette), 8, 9–13
Renoji-dachi (L-stance), 26, 27
Renshi (special title), 107, 108
Reverse-half-facing position, 29
Reversing directions, 32
Rising high block, 40, 68
Round kick, 47

Safety guidelines, 14, 19
Sanbon kumite (three-step sparring), 101
Sanchin-dachi (narrow hourglass stance), 26, 27
Seishin kyōiku (spiritual self-cultivation), 111
Seiza (formal sitting or kneeling position), 11, 12
Self-defense, karate as form of, 2, 4, 21–22
Sempai (seniors), 11–13, 107
Sensei (teachers), 11–13, 107, 112
Shaolin-Tsu (Shaolin fist way), 2
Shihan (master), 107
Shiko-dachi (square stance), 26, 27
Shoulders, warm-up exercises for, 15–16
Shūgyō (physical and mental austerity, 2nd level of training), 111, 113
Side kick, 48
Sideways-facing position, 28
Sparring, 5, 9, 11, 100–5
Speed, and striking power, 24
Spiritual development, 110–13
Sport Experiences
  basic karate techniques, 35
  bowing, 10
  front and back stances, 31
  front-stance turns, 33
  gi (uniform) size, 6
  kata (formal exercises), 72
  kumite (sparring), 104

  stances, 26–27
Ten-No-Kata, 55
  warm-up exercises, 15–17
  wearing of belt, 7
Stances, 22, 24, 25–36, 114
Standing bow, 11
Strength programs, 18
Stretching exercises, 14–18
Striking power, 24
Striking techniques, 115
Subak, 3
Suwari-geiko kumite (seated sparring), 105

Tachikata (stances), 114; see also Stances
Tachirei (standing bow), 11
Tae Kwon Do, 3
Tae Kyon, 2–3
Taikyoku Nidan, 75
Taikyoku Sandan, 75
Taikyoku Shōdan, 72–75
Taisabaki (body shifting), 34
Target areas, of body, 22, 23, 24
Ten-No-Kata (Kata of the Universe), 53–71
Titles, 107, 108
Trunk, warm-up exercises for, 15
Tsugi-ashi (feet sliding), 31
Tsukiwaza (punching techniques), 115; see also Punches

Uchi Hachinoji-dachi (inverted yōi stance), 25, 26
Uchiwaza (striking techniques), 115
Ukewaza (blocking techniques), 115–16; see also Blocks
Uwagi (jacket), 5, 6

Warm-up exercises, 14–18
Warrior, code of the, 110–11
Weapons, body parts as, 19–21, 24
Wrists, warm-up exercises for, 16

Yōi (ready) position, 25
Yori-ashi (foot-sliding), 31

Zazen (meditation), 12
Zenkutsu-dachi (front stance), 25, 26, 27, 28–29, 32, 56, 57, 58, 59
Zubon (pants), 5